GW00401328

Feeding your child from birth to three

by
Heather Welford

Recipes devised by Mary Whiting and
Fiona Wilcock

Throughout the book, 'baby' has been used wherever possible to prevent overusage of 'he or she'. Where this becomes clumsy, 'she' or 'her' has been chosen but please substitute 'he' or 'his' if your new baby is male!

First published in 1994. This edition 1996.

Health Education Authority
Hamilton House
Mabledon Place
London WC1H 9TX

ISBN 1 85448 908 9

Printed by The KPC Group, London and Ashford

Main text: © Heather Welford 1996
Recipes: © Mary Whiting, 1994 and Fiona Wilcock, 1996

Heather Welford has asserted her right under the Copyright, Designs and Patents Act 1988 to be identified as author of this Work.

Acknowledgements

Thanks to the many parents who have talked to me about their babies and the way they've fed them – not just during the preparation of this book, but in the years I have spent as a breastfeeding counsellor and tutor with NCT, and as a journalist writing about the topic of feeding.

I'd also like to thank Caroline Bunker, writer and cook, who helped with many of the food ideas, Mary Whiting and Fiona Wilcock, who devised the recipes, Karen Ford and Lynn Stockley of the Health Education Authority who read the manuscript, and Dr Petra Clarke at the Department of Health who checked the final text for nutritional accuracy.

Heather Welford
1996

Contents

1 Setting the scene

Feeding your child is more than just a way of getting enough healthy nourishment into her, although that's part of it, of course. Feeding is also a way of getting close to your baby, right

'I want to give my baby the best start in life, and to make sure he gets to eat the right foods. But I get confused with the all the advice on offer, and what other people tell me...'.

from the start. And just a short while later, you'll find eating together means you can both enjoy friendly, sociable, entertaining mealtimes, while your son or daughter discovers new tastes, textures and skills.

It's a shame that feeding in the early weeks, months and years can cause problems and get in the way of the closeness and the fun. Usually, there's a simple solution to these problems. Sometimes a small change of behaviour, technique or approach is all that's needed to put things right.

You'll find some of these suggested changes in this book, plus up-to-date guidance on what's safe, healthy and appropriate for your child to eat.

ARE THERE ANY RULES?

In fact, there are very few rules about what to give your child to eat and drink. They are based on what we know about the way children are able to digest their food, and what we know about the nutrients they need for growth and health.

This area of knowledge does change from time to time. We know a good deal more than we used to about breast milk, for example, and artificial baby milks on sale today have changed a lot even since the 1970s.

We know, too, that adults need a rather different diet from children. That doesn't mean young children should always eat 'special' foods, made just for them. It does mean that while today's adults are encouraged to switch to a 'high-fibre low-fat' diet, children under five, on the whole, don't need to follow the same road.

Growing children need the calories and vitamins in fat, for example. A diet that has a lot of fibre in it may be difficult for a very young child to digest. A lot of fibre may also mean that the child does not get enough calories because of the bulkiness of the food. So the guidelines for a healthy diet for children, few as they are, don't apply to everyone. They also change as the child grows, and widens the range of foods eaten.

WHAT DOES YOUR NEW BABY NEED?

A baby in the womb gets its food through the umbilical cord. The blood in the cord is a complex cocktail of essential nutrients, filtered from the mother's blood, and the cord takes these directly into the baby's body.

At birth, if your baby's healthy, and not born very early, a strong sucking reflex from the very start will help establish breast-feeding. A baby won't need or take large amounts of milk for the first few days. The colostrum made by the breasts up until day three or so after the birth is highly concentrated, with a greater proportion of protein, and a lower proportion of fat, than mature breast milk (the term used to describe the milk made after colostrum). In fact, many babies are quite sleepy at first; their appetite perks up as colostrum is replaced by the mature milk.

Breast milk is the ideal food for all young babies. Pre-term babies may need more than breast milk at first in order to grow satisfactorily. Colostrum and breast milk give your baby the pro-tection against infection she needs to arm her immune system against the new challenges of the outside world.

When breast milk isn't available, for whatever reason, your baby should have a special artificial baby milk, usually based on cow's milk and sometimes called baby milk, or infant formula. This is processed cow's milk, modified to make it more digestible for a new baby, and with a low salt content so that the baby's kidneys aren't overloaded.

OLDER BABIES

From about four months, many babies start showing an interest in foods other than milk.

When the first teeth start to come through, a baby becomes more adept at picking up objects (including foods) and putting them to the mouth. These signs are thought to coincide with the time babies are beginning to be ready for something else. At the same time, the immune system is becoming stronger, and older babies are less susceptible to the sorts of infections they might contract from other foods.

Current UK guidelines say most babies are ready for solid food at some time between four and six months of age.

Older babies need more iron, more calories and more vitamins and minerals. Their digestive system can cope with different proteins. It is thought that giving foods before the body is able to cope properly can lead to food intolerance or allergy.

TODDLERS

Over the next year or so, after the first introduction of solids, healthy babies benefit from increasing their range of foods. A wide variety of foods is important: fruit and vegetables, as well as meat, fish or pulses (peas, beans, lentils); dairy foods, as well as bread, chappattis, rice or pasta; and so on. However, because their kidneys are still maturing, and because babies and toddlers can't yet clearly ask for a drink when they're thirsty, you should avoid adding salt to your child's food. Avoid highly spiced or salted foods until after your child's first birthday.

It's also a good idea to protect your child's teeth from decay by keeping sugary foods as part of the meal, by not sweetening foods and by encouraging a liking for unsweetened foods (see p. 56). Water or very diluted fruit juice should be offered as a drink.

And that's it as far as the dietary rules go. You'll find more detailed advice in the other chapters in this book. There are also suggestions and guidelines on keeping your baby's mealtimes healthy and enjoyable. There are 13 pages of recipes and suggestions for you to try, beginning on p. 86.

2 Breastfeeding

'Breastfeeding was very important to me. I just knew it felt right. I got a real sense of achievement from it. It felt really good to say 'breast' when people asked me how I was feeding him. We carried on until he was 10 months, when I went back to work.'

Many mothers want to breastfeed their babies, mainly because they're aware of the fact that human milk is the ideal food for baby humans. It would be astonishing if nature hadn't arranged it like this. Breast milk has evolved with the human race over millions of years; every mother produces breast milk, simply because of the combined hormonal effect of being pregnant and giving birth. Even today, with breast milk substitutes (bottles, teats and formula baby milk) available in most parts of the world, most babies are nourished at the breast and never receive manufactured baby milks at any stage.

BREAST MILK

Breast milk is made up of fat, protein, sugar, plus a highly complex collection of vitamins, enzymes and minerals, and trace elements, some of which are still being discovered. It arrives direct from you to your baby, and contains exactly what she needs in food and drink for the first months of life.

Breast milk contains special fats called long chain lipids, which nourish the developing brain and retina (the seeing part of the eye). These fats are not present in cow's milk nor in most baby milks.

The protein in breast milk is just right for your baby's digestion. Cow's milk protein contains much larger curds and so cow's milk needs to be modified when being used in the manufacture of baby milks.

The minerals such as iron, zinc, calcium which are essential for your baby's growth, are absorbed several times more efficiently from breast milk than from cow's milk or artificial milks.

As well as nourishing your baby and helping her develop and

grow, breast milk protects against illness and allergy. It does this because it has powerful immunological ingredients in it, including antibodies and enzymes. We're still learning about some of them. These fill the gaps in the baby's own fledgling immune system and help build up a resistance to the germs all around us, and so stay healthy through those vulnerable first months.

Breastfeeding offers protection against:

o   ear infections.

o   gastro-enteritis.

o   respiratory diseases.

This protection lasts throughout baby and toddlerhood, even after breastfeeding has stopped. In the UK, these conditions aren't normally life-threatening to otherwise healthy babies, of course, but they can cause a great deal of discomfort, misery and stress, and they are causes of medical intervention, and hospital admission, in the first year or so of life. Other more serious conditions may also be guarded against, including reducing the risk of childhood diabetes.

Mothers who breastfeed may also reduce their risk of developing breast cancer before the menopause.

Breastfeeding is convenient:

o   there are no bottles and teats to sterilise.

o   there is no powder to dilute.

o   there are no feeds to warm up.

o   you don't need to worry about taking feeding equipment with you when you go out.

o   there is no problem in a domestic crisis like a power cut when you can't boil water for a feed.

o   and it's free!

Quite apart from these health advantages, breastfeeding is a lovely thing to do for your baby! It's enjoyable and relaxing for you (it stimulates the release of calming, soothing hormones) and many mothers say how good they feel, watching their baby grow so healthily, and feed contentedly

'The worst thing about breastfeeding is the conflicting advice you get. I heard everybody's pet theory about breastfeeding and I could have got very confused. Even when things were obviously going well, I found people tended to blame the milk every time my baby cried.'

When breastfeeding is difficult, or doesn't get going very soon, it can be upsetting. You may even feel you're failing as a mother in some way. Most problems can be overcome, with the right help and information. If you find yourself concerned about anything, seek help from a midwife, health visitor or breastfeeding counsellor. Contact a breastfeeding counsellor through one of the organisations listed on p.98.

Breastfeeding isn't always an instinct; we have to learn how to do it, like any other skill. In the past, little girls learnt the easy way, by watching their mothers, neighbours, friends and relatives feed their babies. But today, the sight of a baby being breastfed is a comparative rarity, and we're at a real disadvantage. We have to learn by doing – and in today's world, it helps quite a lot with our confidence if we understand what we're doing, and why.

HOW BREASTFEEDING WORKS

Before the birth

The breasts start preparing for making milk as soon as you conceive. Nature, of course, assumes your baby will need and take your milk, and gets to work accordingly. Some mothers notice breast changes straightaway, even before they've even missed a period.

The nipples develop prominent little spots, for a start. These are the openings of tiny glands, called Montgomery's tubercules, which secrete an oily substance that keeps the nipples soft and flexible. This, incidentally, is why creams sold to 'prepare your nipples for feeding' are redundant. You do the job yourself quite adequately.

Inside, the fatty tissue that gives the breasts their shape and fullness starts being replaced by milk producing and storing cells. Your breasts may seem larger, and feel more tender to the touch than before.

In late pregnancy and in the first days after the birth

This is when your breasts produce something called colostrum. Compared to mature breast milk (produced after the colostrum, around day three or four onwards) it's low in fat and high in protein. It's especially rich in antibodies, so it protects the brand new baby from the range of bacteria encountered for the very first time on the outside. It also has a laxative effect, helping to clear the baby's gut of meconium (the first bowel movements).

Colostrum is produced in small quantities, which normally suits the new baby, who doesn't want or need much at this stage. And, athough it's small in amount, it's the most important part of the nourishment and protection a baby needs in the first few days of life. The appearance of colostrum is sometimes described in books as 'straw-coloured', but it can range from being like golden syrup to dark orange in colour. It usually has a translucent, shiny quality that differs from the rather creamier appearance of mature breast milk.

The initial production of mature milk is called 'the milk coming in'. It happens whether or not you have put your baby to the breast.

The more your baby feeds, the more milk you'll make

Your body needs to be told to go on producing breast milk, or else production stops or slows down. It's your baby who issues the order to continue making it, simply by feeding.

The very action of sucking at the breast does several important things: it fills the baby's stomach with the milk (of course); it sends an impulse to the mother's pituitary gland at the base of the brain, which in turn produces oxytocin, a hormone which makes the breasts release the milk stored in the storage cells deep in the breast (this release is called the let-down reflex); it sends a further message to the brain, which then 'tells' the breast to replace the milk that's removed, just as if your baby is putting in an order for the next meal at the same time as consuming this one.

In fact, the whole system works rather like a state-of-the-art supermarket checkout: as the till registers you've bought baked beans, it sends a computerised order to the warehouse, to replace the can on the shelves with another one. The more cans we the customers buy, the more cans come from the warehouse. And the more your baby feeds, the more milk you'll make. Mothers of twins and triplets can make enough milk, because two or three times the sucking means two or three times the milk.

Trying to limit your baby's time or frequency at the breast is a recipe for a poor supply. Allow your baby to suck when she wants to, and you will build up a supply to match her needs. It's unhelpful to keep your baby waiting longer between feeds because you think you'll have made more if you space the feeds out. To keep the supermarket analogy going, when customers start buying fewer cans of baked beans, the purchasing department decides to stop stocking that product altogether!

The most effective stimulation happens when your baby has a good mouthful of breast. If she's sucking the nipple only, rather as one would suck on a bottle teat, it will be harder to take sufficient milk, the let-down reflex may not work quite so well, and the milk-removal won't be as good as it should be. At worst, this situation produces a hungry baby, a poor milk supply and agonisingly sore nipples. We'll see how to get this right on p.9.

HOW TO BREASTFEED

Getting going – the early days of breastfeeding

Virtually every woman is physically capable of making enough milk to breastfeed her baby, but that's not the whole story. She needs the right information, and friendly, supportive encouragement as well.

Try and feed your baby as soon as you can after delivery. This means straightaway, unless you or your baby have any problems that need to be dealt with by the medical or midwifery staff.

If you can't feed your baby at that time, don't worry. It's far from crucial to breastfeeding success. It can mean an easier start, however, as many babies are especially alert and responsive in that first hour. Don't worry, either, if there's not much sucking done at this very first feed. Many babies use the time to lick, smell, taste and look rather than feed – and that's okay. It's all part of the process of getting to know you, which will help make you familiar next time you offer a feed.

Ask a midwife to help you position your baby. You'll need to make sure you're comfortable, too, so ask for extra pillows if you feel you need them.

Bringing your baby to the breast

Follow these points at every feed. They're important to make sure you don't get sore, and to allow your baby to get a good feed and stimulate your milk supply.

○ Hold your baby on her side, across your body, chest to chest. For most people, the easiest way is to support the baby with your forearm. If you are offering the left breast, hold the baby on your left arm, head towards your elbow, feet towards your hand. There are other positions you might prefer instead.

○ Change the baby's position a little, if you have to, to make sure she can reach your breast without having to turn or flex the head up or down. It should be effortless! You may need to raise your baby on a pillow at first, and possibly to support your breast with the flat of your hand as well as, or instead of, the pillow (this would be your right hand if the baby is in the position outlined above).

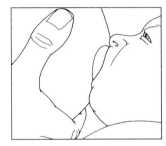

○ If your baby is keen to feed, she'll open her mouth. When it's wide (as wide as a yawn), with tongue thrust well forward, bring the baby onto your breast. 'Aim' so your nipple is towards the roof of the baby's mouth. This way, the nipple and a good lot of breast tissue will be taken in, with the tongue underneath and out. This is called 'latching on'. When your baby is well latched on, both tongue and jaws can literally 'milk the breast', squeezing the milk out, and taking it to the back of the throat to swallow it.

None of this should hurt. If it does, take your baby off (by breaking the suction with a finger inserted between your breast and the baby's mouth) and try again.

Ask for help whenever you feel you need it. If you're at home, ask the community midwife to check your positioning for you. Breastfeeding counsellors (see p. 98) can also help.

It may be difficult at first

Don't be too concerned if your baby seems difficult to feed at first. You may need to be quite patient, getting in a lot of practice at feeding in these early days. Don't feel you have to give up if your baby cries and yet won't take the breast. This can be very upsetting for you, but in most cases, if you try to relax, soothing and calming your baby before trying to feed at the breast again, the problem resolves itself. Some breastfeeding counsellors have found that giving the baby a finger or two to suck calms them down so they sleep, and then wake up ready to latch on without any more problems.

How long?

Let your baby stay on the first breast you offer for as long as she seems to want; then, offer the second side. Some babies only ever take one side at a feed, and others always have both. Some chop and change. Whatever happens, it's best to leave it to your baby to decide. It will seem difficult at first, but you'll soon learn to understand your baby's responses.

Take care to avoid common pitfalls:

- Don't post your nipple into her partially-open mouth.

- Don't let the baby suck the nipple in as if it was a straw.

- Don't hold your baby on her back, as if you were about to bottle feed.

- Don't get your fingers or thumb in the way of the nipple

- Don't press on your breast to keep it away from your baby's face, because you're worrying the baby can't breathe. Babies' noses are snub, designed for easy breathing while feeding. If you feel your breast is smothering your baby, support your breast from underneath.

- Don't stroke your baby's cheek to make her turn her head to breastfeed. This can be confusing for her, and in any case, there shouldn't be any need.

- Don't push your baby onto the breast with a hand on the back of the head. Don't let anyone else do this, either. This sort of treatment frightens some babies and makes them reluctant to take the breast at future feeds.

Leaving it up to your baby can be important, because only they know whether they've had enough. The breast releases watery 'fore-milk' first, when your baby begins to suck. This is at the front of the breast, stored for easy access just behind the nipple and areola. Then, as the feed gets underway, the let-down reflex (see later) releases the fattier, satisfying 'hind-milk' stored more deeply inside the breast. Letting your baby have as much as is needed gives a good feed, making her feel full and happy.

Wind

Babies always take in air as they feed, some more than others. After a feed, gentle back rubbing with your baby lying against your shoulder or held a little forward on your lap may bring up some wind that would be uncomfortable otherwise. There may not always be anything to come up. Sometimes a small amount of milk comes up. This is called 'posset' and it's perfectly normal.

Feeding patterns

After two to three days, your baby may want to feed frequently day and night: 10 or 12 feeds a day isn't uncommon, and each feed may seem to last a long time. Your baby may not be feeding all that time; instead, your baby may come off and on the breast, wriggle, cry, splutter, seem to fall asleep and then wake up. All this can make a feed last about an hour. Other babies are more business-like from the start. Most babies will have the occasional hard-to-feed session, or odd day when nothing seems to keep them happy for long.

Feeding in front of others

Mothers are sometimes made to feel embarrassed if they breastfeed their babies in a public place. They may even feel awkward breastfeeding at home, in front of other people. Somehow or other, our notion of the breast as sexual has meant breastfeeding is seen by some to be an exhibitionist act. This is a great shame. If you want to breastfeed, but feel uncomfortable doing so in public, wearing tops that pull up means no one can see very much at all.

'I thought I'd be so embarrassed, especially feeding in front of people like my father-in-law. At first, I used to go into another room. But then I grew more confident about it. After all, if people are uncomfortable about a mother doing the most natural thing in the world for her baby, that's their problem, not mine!'

Getting established – the early weeks of feeding

If your baby is around the three-week stage, and feeding still seems very unsettled and unrewarding, don't feel nothing is ever going to go right with breastfeeding. However, do persist in trying to get help.

It may well be that the position of your baby on the breast still needs some correcting. If you've been giving bottles (for whatever reason) your baby may be confused about how to feed. You may need support and help with phasing out the bottles, so that the baby learns that milk comes from breasts again. You'll find more information on unsettled babies on p. 21.

Babies who are becoming well-established on the breast latch on, suck and swallow well, getting stuck in with no messing around at most feeds. They're likely to feed less frequently, too.

As time goes on, you may notice that some feeds seem very short. Some babies want to come off after just a few minutes; babies who have always needed both sides at a feed only want one. Your breasts may feel softer than before.

This is all normal, and can happen at any time from about three weeks on. It's actually a sign your breast milk supply, and the baby's needs, are responding to each other.

At first, when breastfeeding is just getting underway, production of milk is helped by high levels of the hormone prolactin, which circulates in every recently-delivered mother's body. Researchers have found that prolactin levels fall in the subsequent months, and by six months, they're back to pre-childbirth levels. Instead, milk production relies much more on the very act of feeding. If your baby feeds, you make milk just as at the beginning, but now you make it more quickly, and you make it more efficiently.

Most babies develop some sort of feeding routine as the weeks go by. Many babies still have an unsettled time each day, however, often in the evening. This happens whether or not your baby is breastfed. Your baby may be on and off the breast a lot, only settling for short periods before crying again. You'll probably find your baby grows out of this in time, and in any case, you can try to bring on more peaceful evenings by making a routine of feed, bath, feed. This is always worth trying if you have a baby of three months or so who still wants several short feeds each evening (see p. 12).

Most older babies feed between five and eight times a day.

Combining breast and bottle

If you plan to breastfeed, you should try to avoid any bottles of milk in the early days – even an occasional one can interfere with the learning process for you and your baby.

The bottle of formula is likely to fill your baby up, so a breast-feed is missed, and your supply is stimulated less. Just as impor-tantly, if your baby starts to learn about bottle feeding before developing breastfeeding skills, the baby can find the breast con-fusing. It's then difficult to latch her on to the breast.

Some babies can develop both sorts of sucking skills, without any problem. Others learn one at the expense of the other. Breastfed babies who have any bottles at all in the first week are three times as likely to be fully bottle fed by the end of the next week.

The safest option is not to offer a bottle at all, unless you really have to or until you're confident of your milk supply and of your baby's ability to latch on. There seems no need to give a bottle in preparation for going back to work.

However, some mothers, understandably, prefer to reassure themselves on this, and give their babies bottles before the very last day of maternity leave.

If you want to give your baby a bottle, it seems to help if someone other than yourself gives it. The baby may be less con-fused.

If you plan on stopping breastfeeding, and switching to the bottle, do it gradually. Suddenly stopping after fully breastfeeding can cause engorgement, blocked ducts and mastitis. Instead, you can substitute one breastfeed with a bottle feed, doing away with one feed every two days, so the complete switch takes place over 10 or 15 days. Or, you can top your baby up with, say, 50 ml of formula milk after each breastfeed. Both these methods allow your supply to run down evenly and slowly. In fact, many mothers who actually don't want to stop breastfeeding find they get manoeuvred into doing so by topping up or supplementing with formula milk, perhaps because they feel they don't have enough breast milk. Do this often enough, and you may well not have sufficient breast milk.

You don't have to make any special effort to combine breast and bottle, or breast and cup, if you've been breastfeeding happily for a few months. After this length of time, breastfeeding is so well-established, many mothers find they can keep a supply going on just one feed a day, if that's what suits them and their babies.

Express yourself!

You may want to express your breast milk for a number of reasons:

○ because your baby is ill, or pre-term (see p. 18), and unable to come to the breast.

○ because you need to be away from your baby at a time when you would normally feed, and you don't want her to have formula instead of breast milk.

○ because you need to be away from your baby for an extended time, and want to maintain your breast milk supply.

In addition, some babies have a special difficulty in sucking at the breast because of a condition like cleft lip and palate, or Down's syndrome, but may manage a bottle with a teat. You can also use expressed milk to prepare dry foods, like baby rice.

For information on expressing right from the start, to establish a milk supply, see p. 16.

You can use a pump to express the milk or your hands. Pumps come in two main sorts: hand pumps and electric ones. Most hospitals have an electric pump, and you can hire similar models for home use. You can buy smaller pumps which work on the mains or with batteries. Generally, hand pumps are a lot cheaper to buy than electric ones. You can express at any time which suits you.

You won't be 'pinching' the milk from your baby, as express-ing stimulates your supply. Most women find that they only get a small amount of milk out at first, and they may need to express several times before they get enough for a full feed. Some women get very skilled at it, though, and can take off as much as they need quite quickly without difficulty.

It seems to help if you 'think baby' when you're expressing, and make an effort to relax and be comfortable.

Checkpoints for expressing milk

o   **Relax and be comfortable.**

o   **Keep your expressing equipment clean.**

o   **Keep the milk in the fridge or freezer.**

o   **Use gentle pressure and don't pinch the nipple when hand expressing.**

Make sure all your expressing equipment is clean (by sterilis-ing) and keep each expression of milk in the fridge. You can add the next expression to the ones you've already done, if you're expressing over a day. After 24 hours it should all go in the freezer, labelled and dated, in a freezer-proof container (some mothers use ice cube trays, which makes defrosting small amounts easier).

Hand expressing only needs a clean, sterilised bowl and a clean pair of hands. Experiment until you find the most effective movements to get the milk out. It seems to help if you gently stroke the breast towards the nipple first. Then, two-handedly, with your thumbs on top and the flat of your hands underneath, slightly raise the breast and push gently inwards. Use gentle pres-sure from your thumbs, stroking towards the nipple, to ease the milk out; don't pinch the nipple ends!

Expressing is going well if you get a 'let-down' – the reflex action that causes the milk to be released from the storage cells, which you'll see as a spurting, and sometimes even a continuous flow of several seconds.

How much?

It may be trial and error at first but you'll soon get to know how much your baby will take. As a rough guide, assume 2½ oz of milk per pound of body weight in 24 hours. So, a 10 lb baby will take 25 oz of milk a day (about 4-6 oz a feed).

WORKING AND BREASTFEEDING

Yes, it can be done. In some countries, such as Brazil, breastfeeding mothers are given paid time to leave their desks or benches to breastfeed. In others, such as Sweden, good maternity leave arrangements allow mothers to return to their jobs well after the time when a baby would be exclusively breastfed. In the UK, however, if you go back to work after having a baby, it could well be between six weeks and three months, when your baby is on milk alone.

You can choose among a range of options if you want to continue breastfeeding (and some mothers decide to wean on to formula milk when they go back to work):

- breastfeed your baby when you're with her; have the minder give a bottle of formula milk when you're not. The body responds well to fluctuating demands (such as full breastfeeding at weekends, and partial on the week) once breastfeeding is established.

- breastfeed your baby when you're there and express for the times you're not, with the minder giving EBM (expressed breast milk) in a bottle.

- a combination of the two, using EBM when it's available, and formula when it's not.

If you're working full-time, you will almost certainly need to express milk at work, and save it in a fridge. Take it home in a cool bag.

It can be quite a commitment to express in these circumstances, but it's not likely to last long, unless you go back to work very early. Most babies can take some of their fluids from a cup from about four months, which is when you might start thinking about introducing solids.

PRE-TERM BABIES

Babies born before week 36 of pregnancy (the generally-accepted definition of pre-term) may have problems sucking and swallowing at the breast.

You'll need to discuss your baby's feeding needs with the paediatrician. There are differences among experts as to the best way to feed a pre-term baby, although there are definite benefits if your baby gets some breast milk. Pre-term milk may be small in quantity, but it's highly concentrated in nutrients and antibodies. The paediatrician may feel your baby needs extra nutrients and may advise a top up with a special pre-term formula, but this shouldn't stop you moving on to full breastfeeding later.

It's harder to establish breastfeeding with a pre-term baby, and the earlier your baby's born, the harder it can be. You need to express your breast milk by hand or with a pump several times a day – every three to four hours, and once at night. This can then be given in the tube if the baby is tube fed, or from a tiny cup, held up to the mouth so that your baby can lap it up with tongue and lips.

Babies born before week 34 or thereabouts, may not have a good sucking reflex, and may find it especially hard to co-ordinate all the mouth and jaw actions used in feeding.

Hold your baby close whenever you can, and offer your breast even if she's sleepy and not interested. The skin-to-skin contact is helpful, and it's all part of getting to know you, and building up a familiarity with your touch, smell and taste.

Sometimes, pre-term babies are sleepy and lethargic. Then, when they start to catch up they act like any other newborn – they may be restless and hungry much of the time. This doesn't mean you can't have enough milk. It means you need to make more, by feeding more often. You'll need extra support and encouragement during this time.

IF YOU'VE GOT A PROBLEM

Breastfeeding mothers often give up because they hit a difficulty and don't know how to overcome it. Most problems do have solutions. A breastfeeding counsellor, a midwife or a health visitor should be able to help you. If anyone says the answer to your difficulty is to give the baby a bottle of formula milk, then get a second opinion. It's so rarely the only option.

Soreness

Tenderness that gets better, rather than worse, over the first few days of feeding, isn't especially worrying, but nipple soreness, especially increasing soreness, isn't normal. It usually means your baby isn't getting on the breast in a way that allows sucking and swallowing without hurting you. Get your positioning checked, and read p. 9 again.

Thrush

Thrush (candidiasis) is another cause of sore nipples. Suspect this if you've had time feeding when you weren't sore. Your baby may or may not have symptoms of thrush (white deposits) in the mouth. Either way, you both need to be treated by your general practitioner (GP) to prevent the thrush recurring between you.

'Sore nipples are miserable – I wouldn't wish them on anyone. Things got better after I asked the midwife to help me get Joshua repositioned ... but he still took a few days to learn how to do it right every time. It was worth it, though.'

Thrush can also affect the breasts. You'll feel it inside the breast, sometimes as a sharp, shooting pain. Again, both you and your baby need medical treatment.

Engorgement

Sore breasts can be caused by engorgement, that uncomfortable, over-full feeling that may happen when your milk comes in, especially if your baby hasn't been feeding very much. You can soften your breasts, by expressing a little milk, to make it easier for your baby to latch on.

Blocked ducts

A blocked duct can also cause soreness. This happens when milk gets 'stuck' in one part of the breast and forms a plug. You can recognise it by a red patch on your breast, and there may also be a lump there too. You can sometimes massage it away while your baby is feeding. Check your clothing, or the way you hold your baby, isn't pressing on your breast and causing a blockage.

Mastitis

Mastitis, an inflammation or infection in the breasts, can follow a blocked duct. It can also (more rarely) be caused by a bug (perhaps from the baby's nose) entering the breast through the nipple. You may feel sore, achy and miserable, as if you have flu. See your GP for advice. You may be given antibiotics if it's thought there's an infection there. Gentle massage and hot and cold compresses can ease the discomfort. For a hot compress, wrap a hot water bottle in a towel and hold it against the affected part. For a cold one, use a pack of frozen peas in a towel.

Getting help

Breastfeeding counsellors know a lot about treating and preventing blocked ducts and mastitis. Get in touch if you feel you have a problem that's not going away, or one that keeps recurring. See p. 98 for how to contact one near you.

Crying, unsettled baby

This can be a feeding problem, though not always. It's almost always perceived as one, which is very undermining if you want to breastfeed.

If the crying gets better or stops, when you feed your baby, then do so. Babies have only one way of telling you they need comfort or food, and that's by crying. Leaving them uncomforted doesn't teach them to be 'good', but it could teach them the miserable lesson that no matter how distressed they are, no one will come to help. Let your baby stay as long as needed on the first breast before offering the second, so your baby is able to take as much of the fatty milk (which comes later in the feed) as appetite dictates.

You may need help in coping with a baby who is difficult to settle, as even feeding doesn't always keep a miserable baby happy. Someone else can give a cuddle until your baby is asleep, before putting the baby to bed. Crying is sometimes described as colic, especially if it happens for prolonged periods, and every day.

There has been some suggestion, backed up by a small amount of research, that traces of dairy products in the mother's milk can cause a colicky reaction in susceptible babies. The same is true of mothers who drink a lot of coffee, tea or cola, or who eat a lot of chocolate.

Cutting these items out of your diet is worth a try (as long as you don't go short of nutrients, which you might if you went for a long time without any dairy products), but you do need to try it for several days before you can be sure whether it makes a difference to your baby's restlessness and crying (or not).

There's no good evidence that you should cut anything else out, still less deliberately avoid them in the first place.

Unexplained, regular prolonged crying does need checking out medically, to rule out any underlying problem. Your GP may suggest some anti-colic medicine, or you can buy some preparations over the counter at the pharmacist.

YOUR QUESTIONS ANSWERED

How long should I breastfeed my baby?

As long as you and your baby like. Breastfeeding can go on with advantage (compared to giving ordinary milkman's milk or infant formula) for a year, and many mothers and babies choose to go on beyond that.

Can I breastfeed when my baby has teeth?

Yes. Some babies give their mothers a bite every so often, more in play or frustration than anything else. Usually, a firm but gentle 'no' puts a stop to it. In normal breastfeeding, the teeth aren't used at all.

Is breastfeeding a contraceptive?

Yes and no. Full breastfeeding has a strong contraceptive effect, as it suppresses ovulation, but few UK mothers would want to rely on this, as you may not get any warning when ovulation, and your fertility, return. It's unusual, though not unknown, to have periods when you're fully breastfeeding.

Will breastfeeding change the shape of my breasts?

Everyone's breasts change in pregnancy, and again when the milk comes in. In the early weeks, breastfeeding may make your breasts larger and firmer, too. Then when you stop breastfeeding, after whatever length of time, it can take a while for the breast milk-making and storage tissue to be replaced by fat. It will return, however. You may never look or feel quite the same as you were, but that's far more to do with getting older and with having babies, than with breastfeeding itself.

Can I change my mind if I want to breastfeed my baby after a period of bottle feeding?

Possibly. Your body will produce milk again, given the right stimulus of a sucking baby, but not all babies want to co-operate. Some mothers manage to 'relactate', as it's called, with the help of a nursing supplementer, a device which gives formula milk to the baby through a tube that's attached (with a plaster) to the nipple, so the baby sucks both tube and nipple. The baby gets a reward for sucking (the reward is the milk) and stimulates the supply in the breasts at the same time. Ask a breastfeeding counsellor where you can get one.

How do I know my baby's getting enough milk?

If babies gain weight, develop well, wet nappies, and seem content after most feeds, then they're getting enough. If your baby doesn't thrive in this way, then get your positioning checked, make sure you're allowing your baby to feed often (to build up your supply) and let her stay on the first side for as long as she wants.

Is it possible for a breastfed baby to become constipated?

Because breast milk is the perfect food for young babies, it is very rare for a breastfed baby to become constipated. The stools of a breastfed baby are yellow, soft and easy to pass. However, you may notice your baby goes several days between opening her bowels. This is normal. It's also normal for babies to open their bowels very often – some babies do it every time they're fed. A wide range of patterns is normal.

Do I need to drink or eat anything special while I'm breastfeeding?

No. Eat according to hunger, drink according to thirst. It's normal to feel thirsty in the first weeks, sometimes during a feed, but you don't need to make any special effort to drink anything more. The same goes for food. As long as you aren't on a severely limited diet, you'll produce enough excellent quality breast milk for your baby. It's worth your while to look after yourself, by eating well. Looking after a baby is tiring, whether you're breast or bottle feeding. You can keep your energy level higher with good food.

My partner wants to help. What can I suggest?

There are lots of ways your partner can help take care of your baby and, at the same time, get close to her. For example, by comforting, bathing, dressing or changing nappies. Or by feeding the baby with your expressed milk. Otherwise he could support you by doing housework, preparing meals etc. Remember, there's plenty of time later on to get more involved in feeding.

3 Bottle feeding

Bottle feeding generally means giving a young baby formula milk, or infant formula, from a bottle, as opposed to giving breast milk from the breast. Some mothers know from the start of pregnancy (and maybe even before then) that they don't want to breastfeed.

Others long to breastfeed, and start off doing so, only to find they hit problems that make feeding too difficult to cope with. They change to the bottle with feelings of disappointment and, sadly, guilt. Still others give breastfeeding a try, find they don't much like it after all, and then switch. Then, there are mothers who breastfeed for as long as they find it fits in with other demands on their lives, and make the change when they return to work or simply feel the time is right.

'I never felt breastfeeding was an option for me. I knew right from the start that I wouldn't want to do it – I suppose I'm embarrassed at the whole idea of it. So I put Paul on the bottle straight away. I don't regret it. It was better for me to feel happier about feeding, than to force myself to do something I didn't want to do.'

It does seem that the majority make the change with at least some feelings of regret. Of mothers who stop breastfeeding between the ages of six weeks and two months for example, only 3 per cent say they stopped because they'd breastfed for as long as they intended to. We'll look at the feelings that bottle feeding arouses on p. 32.

INFANT FORMULA

What is 'infant formula'?

Infant formula is an artificially manufactured milk, usually based on cow's milk. There's no special biological reason why cow's milk is used, rather than any other mammal's milk. However, western industrial countries also have strong dairy industries, and we can produce a lot of milk fairly readily.

The milk is modified in the factory to make it more digestible for a young baby. Unmodified cow's milk is too high in sodium (salt). Other changes are made, and research goes on to make formula milk less unlike breast milk. Recently, for example, one major manufacturer claimed to be the first to add two 'long chain polyunsaturate' fats to the formula, because they were in breast milk, and not cow's milk. It can't be clear that adding anything to formula makes the substance work the same way as it does in breast milk of course.

A few babies are allergic to the protein in cow's milk, and they need to have a baby milk based on a different protein. The one most widely used is soya protein, taken from the soya bean. This protein is mixed with other nutrients in the manufacture of soya infant formula. Because it isn't derived from milk it is acceptable to vegans.

Only give your baby milk which is specially formulated for babies, and sold as such. At present, only cow's milk formula and soya formula have Department of Health approval for this use. Check with your midwife or health visitor if you're unsure. It's important to check the sell-by date of any pack of formula you're buying. If you stick to well-known names, and buy from a reputable chemist or supermarket, you should avoid problems.

Which brand?

If you start off bottle feeding, it's generally considered to be a good idea to stay with the brand of formula your baby has in hospital. Although in fact, as most hospital milk is ready-to-feed (that is, already made up with water and in the bottle) and the milk you buy is usually powder or granules which you make up at home, you aren't actually giving an identical product. Waters differ from area to area and household to household, and several studies have shown just how inconsistently parents (who are only human, after all) actually make up the feeds.

Bottle-fed newborns generally begin feeding on whey-dominant formula. These are sometimes branded as a 'stage one' formula. It means the major source of protein in the milk is whey. They are closer, in this respect anyway, to breast milk, than casein-dominant formulas, which may be branded as a 'stage two' milk. Most manufacturers have both a whey-dominant formula and a casein-dominant formula in their ranges. Casein is a protein that is thought to take longer to digest, and that's why formulas with this as their main protein are marketed for 'older' babies.

Experts feel there's no firm evidence that casein-dominant formulas are any more 'satisfying' than whey-dominant ones. However, many mothers do make the change in the first weeks, often because they feel their baby is hungry and needs something more filling to keep her happy. If the baby then settles down better on the new milk, it could just be because she was going to get better and more contented anyway, as she got older, or maybe it is the milk. It's always difficult to explain changes in baby behaviour.

Always stick to a recognised infant formula. Babies shouldn't have doorstep milk until at least the age of six months, when it can be mixed with other foods. Stick to formula or breastmilk as a drink for a year.

Follow-on milks

For information on 'follow-on milks', see p. 75.

Dried and ready-to-feed formula

Most parents buy packages of dried formula, making up the feeds with boiled water (see p. 27). An alternative is to buy ready-to-feed formula, in cartons, which you pour straight from the carton into a sterilised bottle.

These feeds are more expensive than the dried formula, but they're handy in emergencies (such as a power cut, or when you've run out of dried formula) or when you're away from home. They're also useful for parents who give the occasional bottle only.

Making up feeds

You'll get full instructions on how to make up a feed with dried milk plus water on every package of formula milk. There'll be some indication of how much you need according to the age and weight of your baby, too. Bear in mind, though, that your baby's appetite may differ from these averaged–out guidelines, and there will be times when your baby needs more, or less, at any one feed.

When making up a feed, you should always:

- Check that all feeding equipment is scrupulously clean. This is normally done by sterilising, following one of three methods (see p. 29). Bottle-fed babies don't get the protection of breast milk's antibodies, and warm milk is a fertile breeding ground for bugs.

- Add the milk to the measured amount of water, and not the other way round. That way you ensure the milk/water proportion is correct: too strong, and your baby could become thirsty, and in extreme cases dehydrated; too weak, and she won't get the nourishment she needs.

You might find it easiest to make up the entire day's worth of feeds all in one go, perhaps in a sterilised jug. Then pour the feed into a bottle as it's needed. Or, you can make up all the bottles and keep it in the fridge.

You need freshly-boiled water to mix the feed. You then need to cool the bottle down before giving it. If you take your bottle from the fridge, you may prefer to warm it up first, by standing it in a jug of hot water (some babies do take their milk cold, however, without minding). Don't warm the bottle in the microwave. The heat may not be even all the way

'I find it easiest to work to a routine – wash and sterilise all the bottles first thing every morning, then make the feeds up and stick them in the fridge until I need them. That way, the whole thing is done in one go.'

through, and it's possible for hot spots in the bottle to scald your baby's mouth and throat.

The 'right' temperature is reached when a few drops shaken onto your wrist or the back of your hand feel neither warm nor cool – body heat, in other words.

EQUIPMENT

Bottles

Bottles are made in a light, easy-to-clean polycarbonate material, marked with graduations. Choose a well-known brand and don't use 'hand-downs' that may be scratched. You can buy disposable ones, made like a plastic bag, used with a rigid holder. These are sold in a roll and you tear off the bags as you need them. You can also get disposable, rigid bottles, complete with teat. You throw the whole lot away after using it once.

Teats

Teats are made from latex rubber or silicone. The latex ones are softer and more flexible; the silicone ones are tougher, and far longer lasting. It's a matter of personal preference which you use. Most babies manage to use either.

Some teats are sold as 'orthodontic' teats, marketed as being more like a nipple in shape and so able to mimic breastfeeding. This, frankly, is not true. The shape of a baby's mouth on the bottle, and the position and movement of her tongue, are completely different, whatever the shape of the teat. Babies, however, do sometimes develop a preference for one sort of teat. This is more likely to be because they're used to that type of teat rather than because it's more like a nipple.

A slit in the side of some teats is supposed to help reduce air swallowing, and to keep the sides of the teat from sticking together after several sucks.

Most teats are sold with different hole sizes, with small holes for a newborn and larger ones for an older baby. If your baby gets frustrated when sucking, it could be because the holes aren't big enough. You can enlarge the existing holes, by nicking the edge of the holes with a razor blade (remember to sterilise again).

Sterilising

It is essential to sterilise feeding equipment up until your baby is at least six months old. Before sterilisation, all bottles and teats should be washed thoroughly in detergent and then rinsed in clean water. Turn teats inside out to make sure there are no milk traces trapped under the rim or in the 'cherry' (rounded end). A bottle brush helps you clean right down to the bottom of the bottles. You can use one of three methods to sterilise your equipment:

Boiling
Bring a large pan of water to the boil on top of your stove and immerse everything you want to sterilise for 10 minutes, keeping the water boiling all the time. Make sure you have no air bubbles trapped inside the bottles, and that everything is underneath the water (teats and dummies can bob up if you're not careful). This method is handy and quick, for the odd bottle and teat. However, if you're doing it every day with several bottles, teats and other bits and pieces, it can be rather a nuisance as it may mean several pan loads.

Steaming
You use an electric steam steriliser for this, kept on your kitchen surface. Most hold a day's worth of bottles plus other items. They look neat, and they're efficient and quick. They cost more than other methods, though most parents feel the convenience outweighs the expense. A variation on this method needs a microwave oven, and a steam steriliser designed for use with it. It's even quicker than electric steaming, and it's a method worth considering if you already have a microwave oven.

Cold water method
You need to buy sterilising tablets or liquid from the supermarket or pharmacist (make sure they are formulated for use with baby's

feeding equipment). These are then dissolved in cold water in a special plastic tank, which can be bought, or in any household plastic food container or bowl. Renew the solution every 24 hours (you can use the stuff for dishcloths before actually throwing it out). Non-metal feeding items soak in it for at last half an hour. You should rinse off the solution with cooled, boiled water before using the items. Don't keep things in it for hours as the long-term soaking rots rubber.

> **Ready for use**
>
> After sterilising, keep items clean and covered ready for use. Teats can be kept in a sterilised jam jar or cup; bottles in a sterilised ice cream container or similar. Keep a clean tea-towel over the whole lot.

GIVING A FEED

When you offer the baby a bottle, hold your baby close, on her back. She'll be more comfortable if she's slightly upright (older babies may prefer to be almost sitting).

- Tilt the bottle as you put it in her mouth, and keep it tilted throughout the feed. The teat is then always full of milk. Every so often, you'll need to take the teat out to allow the sides to become unstuck, and let the milk through.

- Enjoy feeding your baby, she'll get a lot of pleasure from being held closely, and from seeing your face. The contentment she shows as she satisfies her hunger and relishes the rhythmic, satisfying sucking action makes feeding a baby much more than just a means of filling her up.

○ Your baby may need a break every so often to be 'winded'. This means sitting her up to help her get rid of any air bubbles she's taken in with her milk, which could be making her uncomfortable. You may like to rub her back, and to allow her to rest on your shoulder, or to lie her tummy-down across your knee while you do this. There's no physiological reason why this should help her burp, but babies seem to like this sort of soothing contact (you can use these winding actions if your baby's breastfed as well, of course). Don't worry if no wind comes up. It's not essential. It may even be that there's none to come. Sometimes a little milk is brought up at the same time. This is called 'posset' – and it's normal.

Your baby will show she doesn't want any more milk by pushing the teat out with her tongue, by crying, falling asleep, or stopping swallowing. Sometimes, you'll think she's had enough, and then she seems to want more. You won't get it right every time.

Pre-term babies (see also p. 18).

Babies born before about week 36 may not be able to suck from a bottle, and they may need their milk through a nasogastric tube (a thin tubing that goes direct to the stomach via the nose and the oesophagus). An alternative may be to give formula in a cup which even tiny babies can lap from.

Your pre-term baby may need special formula, depending on the paediatrician's advice. It's usual for this to be changed to a normal formula when the baby has made up for her extra-early birth in terms of growth and development.

Some very small babies may need a soft teat, with possibly a shorter length on it. They're likely to take small amounts of formula at any one time, and then need feeding more often. They tend to fall asleep very readily, and need patient coaxing with the teat to carry on feeding.

This is at least partly the reason why it is thought easier for pre-term babies to bottle feed rather than breastfeed. The carer can poke the teat in the mouth and stimulate the sucking reflex by moving the teat around. That can't be done with a breast. However, because the breast has a let-down reflex (see p. 7) which gets the milk out in spurts, a pre-term baby might find breastfeeding easier than bottle feeding, which requires continuous sucking and swallowing. And breast milk is definitely beneficial for pre-term babies.

YOUR FEELINGS

Most babies start off by being breastfed, and end up as bottle fed. There's a range of reasons for that, and only some mothers change over because that's what they planned to do. The result is that many mothers may feel sad at giving up. Books, leaflets and health professionals, reminding them that breast is the best milk for young babies may make them feel guilty, as if they've failed in some way.

Although there are powerful health arguments in favour of breastfeeding, we know the majority of bottle fed babies thrive and develop well.

The problem is that to talk of 'choice' is misleading. You may not feel you have a choice if you aren't enjoying breastfeeding, because it's painful, or demanding, or because family and friends are critical, or make you feel embarrassed.

Your choice is also affected if you feel breastfeeding hasn't gone well. A mother who feels this way may start giving some formula. This reduces her milk supply, and she needs to give more formula... and more. In time, she runs out of milk, the baby rejects the breast and she really has no choice but to bottle feed.

You can always consider relactating if you regret bottle feeding. This means offering the breast to the baby and allowing her to start your supply going again. It's sometimes hard; some babies reject the breast once they're used to the bottle. However, if you want to try, a breastfeeding counsellor will help you (see p. 98).

Coming to terms with your decision to bottle feed means learning to accept the circumstances that led up to it, perhaps understanding why it didn't work out, and refusing to blame yourself. It may mean a promise to try again with another baby. Above all, it means accepting that bottle-fed babies are no less well-loved, and that feeding is only one part of your baby's care.

There are many things we do as parents that don't work out as we want them to; all we can do is our best as we see it at the time. Bottle feeding is the right decision for you, if it suits you and your baby best. That applies whether you bottle feed from the start, and if you change after a period, however long or short, of breastfeeding.

IF YOU'VE GOT A PROBLEM

Parents report as many problems with bottle feeding as there are with breastfeeding. Certainly, a big UK survey reported similar proportions, though the nature of the difficulties were rather different. More bottle-fed babies were sick in the first week or so, for example, and there seem to be more problems with wind.

The sickness and the wind tend to get better over time, as your baby's digestion matures. Speak to your midwife, health visitor or GP, however, and ask them to check your baby over for any underlying problem. If your baby is failing to thrive, it may be that she is allergic to cow's milk formula (see p. 64).

Some babies are very reluctant to take much formula in any one go. Like many breastfed babies, they prefer to feed little and often at first. Again, this is a situation that resolves itself. You may need to be patient, and change your baby's nappy halfway through a feed to wake her up to take some more, for example.

We've already seen (p. 25) that appearing dissatisfied is a common reason for changing formula. There's unlikely to be any harm in this, but talk it over with your health visitor first, in order to check your baby's behaviour doesn't mean anything more serious. It's not thought to be a good idea to chop and change formula; give your baby's system a chance to get used to one.

Some babies get a bit constipated on formula. Talk to your health visitor. A drink of water may help.

Your baby's stools may look greenish at times. Don't worry unless this happens with other symptoms that show your baby could be ill (feverishness, lots of unexplained crying, lethargy, refusal of feeds). In fact, all it usually means in a breast or bottle-fed baby is that the milk has proceeded through the body rather more quickly than usual.

YOUR QUESTIONS ANSWERED

I'm going on holiday abroad with my baby. Should I take enough formula with me?

Some manufacturers' products are the same in every country, with a name change. Others differ slightly. A quick phone call to the makers of your baby's usual formula will help you make your decision. If you can't get what your baby has at home, then it would be best to take enough with you.

How can I make night feeds easier?

You can take up a bottle of formula from the fridge and keep it in a cool place for a few hours until your baby wants it. Then, warm it in a jug of hot water (a flask of hot water kept near you can be poured into a jug to save you boiling water in the night).

4 From milk to mixed feeding

Milk, whether breast or formula milk, will help your baby grow and satisfy her nutritional needs for the first few months of life, but at some point, milk isn't able to provide everything your baby requires. At that stage, your baby is ready for mixed feeding, which means that while much of her nutrition continues to come from milk, her everyday diet is supplemented with other foods. This stage is usually called 'weaning', and foods used in this period are called 'weaning foods'. However, weaning is a confusing term, as it also means the process of winding down breastfeeding, and by extension, it can even mean stopping a child from sucking on a bottle.

'People seemed to expect me to be in a rush to wean Jo onto solids. I've heard conversations when parents have actually boasted about how much food their babies were eating when they were just three months old!'

One of the reasons why milk stops being the full and perfect food is that it's relatively low in iron. Babies start to need more iron at around six months old. Around this time, their digestive systems become able to cope with a wider range of foods, including cereals, meat and vegetables. Their calorie needs increase, as they become more active and energetic and continue to grow.

These are what you might call inward and invisible signs that your baby is ready for other foods; after all, you can't actually see when your baby might benefit from more foods, unless she's very obviously under-nourished and ill, but you can spot the outward and visible ones yourself (see p. 37).

There's a certain logic about giving other foods at around six months of age. It's about this time when babies start to show an interest in other foods, reaching out to pick something off your plate for example. It's the age when babies begin to explore the taste and texture of just about anything; an object held in the hand and studied with the eyes will go straight to the mouth in a few seconds. Babies start to get teeth at any time from around four months on (a few have teeth earlier than this, and the occa-sional baby is even born with one or two). There may be a restlessness after feeds, as if your baby was 'asking' for something more. It's clear that normal developmental changes take place, in readiness for the change of diet.

WHAT DO THE EXPERTS SAY?

The current position of the UK Department of Health, based on expert advice, is that solid food (the term solids or solid food is used to mean any food other than milk) can be introduced to breast or bottle-fed infants between four and six months of age.

The World Health Organization recommends exclusive breastfeeding for four to six months, after which other foods can be gradually introduced. Breastfeeding should continue alongside appropriate other foods up to two years of age or beyond. This policy applies specifically to breastfeeding as part of the WHO's continued emphasis on its short- and long-term health benefits compared to bottle feeding.

Commercial baby food

Commercially-packaged baby food is often branded as being suitable 'from three months', as if that's the time you *ought to* give your baby the food. Remember, most babies of this age don't actually need anything other than breast or formula. Be guided by your baby, and not a packet of food! See also p. 45.

HOW DO YOU KNOW WHEN YOUR BABY'S READY TO START?

Don't feel that four months is necessarily the right time, or that you must wait until six months. Be guided by what your baby seems to want. Starting solids is in any case a gradual process. The first days and weeks are important for your baby to become used to the new experience of varying tastes, textures and ways of feeding, as well as a means of getting different foods into her.

Look for these signs at any time from about four months on:

o Your baby reaches out and tries to take food from you or your plate.

o She finishes a breast or bottle feed and seems to ask for more, yet refuses to be put on the breast again, or to have more formula.

o Her weight is causing concern, perhaps because she's failing to gain adequately. Even here, some babies are better off increasing their milk intake, rather than taking solids, and don't forget that a loss of weight or a poor weight gain can indicate illness or failure to thrive, so check with your health visitor or clinic.

o She can pick objects up with her hands and place them in her mouth for investigation.

o She seems to enjoy a few offerings of solid food while she's on your lap or sitting in her chair.

You'll also need to consider if the timing fits in with your life; perhaps you're returning to work, and you'd like to leave your carer the option of giving a solid meal plus a drink in the middle of the day when you're away, instead of you having to express milk.

Ask your health visitor or your baby clinic what they feel about your baby's readiness for solid food. There's a tendency to assume that everybody wants their baby to progress to this stage as soon as possible. Just make it plain you're in no real rush, and if anyone suggests your happy, hale and hearty thriving baby of three months old ought to be having 'something else' now, tell them there's no real reason to do anything at the moment.

It's worth knowing that health visitors and clinics talking about solid food early on may be simply grabbing the chance to talk to you about it while you're there – after all, parents tend to visit the clinic less often as their babies get older. They're not necessarily implying you're behind schedule.

Disadvantages of giving your baby solids too soon

○ Your baby may be sick or have a stomach pain, unable to digest the new food.

○ Early solids may lead to allergies and food intolerance.

○ Early solids mean less milk, leading to a less than ideal diet, as milk is the best food for young babies.

○ Early solids mean another task added to a busy day.

TYPES OF FOOD

First tastes

If your baby begins solid foods before the age of five months or so, you'll almost certainly have to make food specially for her, and help her to feed from a spoon.

That's not to say your baby can't have many of the same foods as you do, as long as the food is cooked and prepared so she can manage it.

Starter foods need to be:

○ smooth in texture.

○ free of artificial flavourings.

○ without a strong taste.

○ with no added salt or sugar.

Foods you can give a very young baby include very small amounts of puréed or mashed vegetables and fruit. Vegetables include potato, carrot, plantain, yam, swede, turnip. Puréed or mashed fruit include apples (the sweet, dessert kind, not the bitter 'cookers'), pears and bananas. You can also give rice, cooked and then mashed (see p. 41).

'Wait until later foods'

Certain items are thought better left until later on. This is because they may be difficult for a young digestive system to cope with, or because they are considered to be linked with the development of food allergies or intolerance if introduced too early. They are:

- ○ Cereals. (These may contain gluten, a protein that some babies cannot tolerate while young. In a very few cases, this intolerance might persist into toddlerhood and even beyond leading to coeliac disease. Gluten is present in wheat, and of course in any foods containing wheat. These include most flour products, including bread and pasta.)

- ○ Eggs.

- ○ Dairy products, fromage frais, yoghurt, or cheese, for example have a high milk content, which hasn't been modified.

- ○ Citrus fruits (for example, oranges, grapefruit).

- ○ Fatty foods (including cheeses and fried foods).

- ○ Nuts (hard to digest, also allergenic).

- ○ Strong-tasting vegetables (such as chillies).

Preparation of food

Vegetables

When you're preparing vegetables for your baby, don't start peeling and boiling a single carrot or half a potato. Instead, when you're cooking vegetables for you and the rest of the family, don't add salt. Then take out a spoonful for your baby, and purée, mash or blend it, moistening with a little of the cooking water if necessary.

Puréeing or mashing is simple to do. If you would normally cook the item for yourself, then do so for your baby. Cook in unsalted water (if it's for yourself as well, you can add the salt later if you want it). Drain and then mash with a fork. You can pass the food through a sieve to get it finer, if you like, or use a hand or electric blender or whisk. You'll find blenders or food processors are only worth using if you have a lot of food to prepare, perhaps because you intend to freeze some. Otherwise, tiny amounts tend to stick round the blades.

> All vegetables contain vitamins (e.g. vitamin C), minerals and fibre (which prevents constipation). Different vegetables and fruit contain different vitamins and fibre, so it's important to vary the kind you give your baby (see p. 39).

Some vegetables like carrot or potato will be popular with your baby on their own, but stronger flavoured ones like turnip or parsnip may go down better if you blend them with a little mashed potato. Just as you wouldn't care for greens on their own, mixing them with a starchy vegetable like potato or yam will make them more palatable for your baby.

If you're not using the food immediately, cover, cool quickly and store in the fridge until the next meal. (Season the remainder before serving for the rest of the family, if you prefer.)

Fruit

Stewed fresh fruit can be a bit sharp without sugar, but there are plenty of other ways your baby can enjoy fruit. You could try:

○ Peeled and mashed banana, avocado, ripe melon, pear, peach, nectarine, mango.

○ Eating apple (peel off a little of the skin and then scrape the flesh with a teaspoon. It will form a smooth juicy pulp on the spoon. This is a convenient snack to take with you when you go out but don't forget the spoon!).

○ Puréed, stewed, dried fruit like apricots, prunes, peaches with no added sugar.

○ Mashed or puréed canned fruit in natural juice (not syrup).

Avoid fruit with seeds or pips unless you can remove them first.

Rice

An alternative first food that many families use either on its own or with a puréed vegetable or fruit is a gluten-free cereal such as rice.

You can buy specially made 'baby rice' in a packet which you then mix with cooled, boiled water or formula milk, or expressed breast milk. Babies usually accept rice fairly readily, as the taste is bland and the texture is smooth. Look carefully at the labels on packets of baby rice as some have sugar added.

Baby rice may have added vitamins, and some brands are sold under a proprietary name, but you don't have to use these. Because of the way baby rice is manufactured, it is quick, easy and convenient to mix. But ordinary household rice, cooked and then puréed, is fine for your baby as well.

> **Take it slowly**
>
> Offer one or two new foods at a time to your baby. That way, if she shows a strong dislike, or even a physical reaction (such as a rash, a tummy ache, sickness, diarrhoea or constipation), you have a better chance of deciding which food it was, and avoiding it for the time being. You can always try again in a couple of weeks, by which time your baby may be able to cope better.

HOW AND WHEN

Helping your baby take the food

Babies under about six months can't sit comfortably in a high chair. Your younger baby will be happier on your lap, or else sitting in her usual baby chair. Remember your baby will need a bib to keep her clothes clean.

Place a small quantity of the food you're offering on the end of the spoon. See how best your baby takes it. Some babies like to lick or suck the food off the spoon. Others manage better if the spoon is more or less placed in the mouth, and then brought out again, against the roof of the mouth, so the upper gums take off the food (it sounds complicated and awkward, but it isn't at all!).

There's bound to be some mess, as your baby won't be able to cope with some mouthfuls, and the overflow will go down her chin.

You'll soon learn the amount to offer, and the pace you need to offer it at. Many babies really enjoy food, and show their pleasure by making appreciative noises and waving their arms around!

When to offer the food

There's no 'right' time to give your baby a meal. Do it when it seems convenient to you and your family. Try to encourage the social side of eating, by having something yourself at the same time, or by arranging it so your baby's mealtime is at the same time as yours and other family members.

'Mealtimes are fun now Melanie has started to take a real interest in food. I love the way she gets all excited when I put her in her high chair ready for dinner. She waves her arms about and makes high-pitched squeals of delight.'

Your baby will build up to three meals a day over the next few weeks. It makes sense if she has them as breakfast, lunch and tea, so you may want to begin the first tastes at one of these times.

It can be helpful to offer a breastfeed or part of a bottle feed before you give the solid food. This means your baby will be calm and happy, with the edge taken off any hunger or thirst, before the more unfamiliar food is given. You can then finish off the meal with the rest of the milk feed.

If you don't want to do it this way, though, it doesn't matter. Many babies are happy to take their milk, by breast or bottle, after the solid food. If your baby still likes to go to sleep after a milk feed, giving all of it before the solids may not be a good idea, as she may be too tired to be bothered with anything else. If she takes her milk quickly, without wanting to sleep, then a full feed before the solids may be fine.

Here's a suggested 'timetable' for a baby of four to five months, just starting on solid food.

○ *First week*
Breast or bottle feed as you and your baby are used to, with two teaspoons of baby rice offered at lunchtime. After three or four days, increase the amount of baby rice, and add some pureed dessert apple to it.

○ *Second week*
Offer puréed or mashed potato at lunch time, and apple with rice at tea time. Keep portions small at first, and go at your baby's pace. If your baby's keen, you can give larger amounts. Keep up your usual milk feeds. Your baby may drop a feed if she's been feeding often.

○ *Third week*
Give a small amount of oat cereal at breakfast time. Try a different vegetable – say, carrot – at lunchtime. Apple and rice at teatime as before. Breast or bottle feed as before.

○ *Fourth week*
As before, but try a different fruit – for example a pear – with the baby rice. Breast or bottle feeds as before, but you could start aiming at dropping one or two milk feeds if you like. One breast or bottle feed at teatime or lunch time could be swapped for a drink from a cup.
By now, your baby is having three small meals a day, plus extra milk. Work towards offering these meals at a time that fits in with when you eat, so you and your baby can enjoy eating together, at least some of the time.

See p. 54 for suggested menus for older babies, well-established on solid food.

FIRST DRINKS

Breastfed babies don't need anything to drink other than breast milk, which supplies everything the baby needs, even in very hot weather. On hot summer days, you may find your baby needs more feeds at the breast, or you may find you don't notice any change in her demands; either way, she'll get what her body requires.

You may have been encouraged to give your baby drinks of water from very early on, but there's usually no real reason why you should.

Giving water, or anything else, could disturb the 'supply and demand' production of breast milk in the early weeks, and confuse the baby's sucking and swallowing action (if the other fluid is given in a bottle). It's also a nuisance: bottle and teat need to be prepared by sterilising, and the fluid has to be bought, or, if it's water, boiled and cooled.

Bottle-fed babies may be more likely to get thirsty than breast-fed babies, as it's certainly possible to make up feeds which are too concentrated. There seems no reason for arguing that you must give your bottle-fed baby a regular drink of cooled boiled water, except on very hot days, or when you feel your baby is thirsty (she may be restless and hot, though otherwise well).

If you want to, you can buy 'flavoured water', bottled specially for young babies. It has a slight taste (usually of fruit or herbs) which some babies seem to prefer to plain water. Some manufacturers produce granules which you mix with boiled and cooled water to make a flavoured drink. Again, you can use these if you want to, though most have sugar in them which is best avoided.

Unless you really feel your baby needs a drink, you don't need to offer her anything other than milk until the age of mixed feeding, when you may want to encourage her to enjoy other fluids from a cup. Once solids become a more important part of her daily diet, you might expect her to be thirstier at times.

Cups

You don't have to use the usual lidded, spouted baby cup – an ordinary cup held up to her mouth is fine – but a baby cup does mean she's probably able to drink without your help rather sooner.

There are different sizes of spouts available, and you may find your baby prefers one sort over another. As time goes on, though, she'll probably become adept at using whatever you give her.

What can you give your baby to drink?

○   Plain water (boiled and cooled) is fine, if your baby will accept it.

○   Make sure bottled mineral water is suitable for babies (some inform you on the packaging). You still need to boil and cool it before use, to make sure it's hygienic.

○   Otherwise choose a very diluted fruit juice or a sugar-free or low-sugar drink. Low-sugar drinks designed for older children which may contain artificial sweeteners should not be used. Check the label to make sure they don't contain sugar by another name, for example, glucose. UHT juice (the sort you buy in a carton) or fresh juice are both fine. All fruit juice needs to be well-diluted for a young baby – use at least four to five parts of water for one part of juice at first.

BABY FOOD: BOUGHT OR HOMEMADE?

Commercially prepared foods

Virtually all babies these days have at least some specially bought, commercially packaged baby food. Some babies' diets are based almost entirely on these foods, with very little home-prepared meals. But some parents and nutritionists have their doubts about the nutritional value of many baby foods.

The main gripe has been the added sugars that make baby desserts, in particular, very sweet indeed. Some manufacturers print 'no added sugar' on their labels, but the products may still contain fruit syrup, for instance, or other sugars such as dextrose or maltose.

Also, many baby foods have a high water content. This means thickening agents are needed to make the foods less sloppy. The

Advantages of commercial baby food

o Most babies enjoy bought baby foods, and of course they're developed to be enjoyable and tasty. You're unlikely to buy something again if your baby didn't like it the first time.

o Bought baby foods are also prepared without added salt, and without artificial additives such as preservatives or flavourings.

o They're also convenient, and need little preparation to serve. In fact, though you may prefer to heat a 'baby dinner', you could serve it straight out of the jar if you wished. Dried foods only need water to mix them to serving consistency.

thickeners add bulk without food value. However, if you read the labels on baby foods, you can avoid the highly-sweetened varieties, and also the ones with a high water content. Look out for:

o vegetable gum.

o gelatine.

They're both thickeners. Remember the main ingredient of any packaged food is listed first on the label. Not surprisingly, you'll find you pay more for better-quality baby foods.

Homemade

Freshly prepared meals, made with good quality ingredients, are likely to be a good deal cheaper than prepared baby food. Also, most families aim to have their babies eating as part of the family, if not straight away, then certainly in time. Bought baby foods are not really like homemade foods in terms of taste or texture. A bought baby cauliflower cheese will always be the same. But the one you make will differ slightly in many ways, every time you make it – even if it's your speciality and you've made it twice a week for ten years. Getting used to these variations, and accepting them, is part of joining in with the family.

Bought baby foods tend to be smooth and unlumpy – even the 'stage two' or 'junior' varieties which attempt to have some chewable bits in them. Homemade foods are unpredictable in texture; some of their lumps are big, some are small, and they're irregular in shape.

Babies who have little experience of homemade foods from the start may have difficulty in getting used to them. Mothers find they are still giving packets and jars when their babies are 15 or 18 months old, and sometimes even older. These toddlers sometimes literally gag on 'normal' foods, apparently unable to cope with them.

This is a nuisance, and it becomes even more expensive, as one jar of baby dinner made for a nine month old is not going to be enough for a toddler twice that age – who may need two.

So even if you're a fan of commercially-prepared foods, try to give homemade meals at least some of the time. If you want to avoid all commercially-prepared foods, then of course you can do so. Just as it's sensible to reject the idea that homemade foods are always better than bought, you can ignore the implicit message in the marketing of the commercially-prepared stuff that only jars and packets can supply everything your baby needs.

See the recipe section (p. 86) for lots of good and simple ideas the whole family can share in, as well as your baby.

IF YOU'VE GOT A PROBLEM

Both you and your baby may sail through these early stages of a change in feeding without any problems, but there's also a chance you may hit some worries. You can always ask for specific advice at your baby clinic, or see your health visitor about anything you're wondering about.

Some problems may be to do with the way your baby reacts to the new foods. True food intolerance or allergy isn't very common, and many of the adverse reactions shown by babies and young children to food simply disappear as they get older. So if your baby seems to develop a reaction to a certain food, it doesn't necessarily mean she will never be able to eat it.

You can reduce the chance of your baby developing an intolerance, even a temporary one, by delaying the introduction of foods in the list on p. 39. In the main, these foods are known to be more likely to be linked with the development of allergy than other foods. Keeping them until your baby's digestive system has matured a little means she will be better able to cope.

Even so, you may still think you spot a reaction to something as plain and simple as a puréed carrot. You might see a rash, or a sore bottom, or notice a change in your baby's bowel habits with more frequent or less frequent motions (because anything your baby eats or drinks will affect her urine and stools at the other end).

Obviously, if your baby is ill (with vomiting as well as diarrhoea, or a fever), she needs medical attention. Don't simply ascribe things like this to the new foods. But if your baby seems okay apart from these reactions, leave that food for a couple of weeks before trying it again.

You might notice your baby seems to dislike certain foods. She may turn her head to one side, or deliberately spit the food out, or push your hand away. Don't press her to take the food. Starting any sort of battle over food is just not worth it. Encourage her, yes, but if she makes it clear she doesn't want the food on offer, then accept the fact calmly, and without showing irritation.

Some babies seem slow to take to solid food. They may appear to dislike whatever you give them, or they cry when you give them something on a spoon. It could be that a baby showing this sort of behaviour is just not ready for solid food. If this happens with your baby, wait a while, say another couple of weeks, before trying again.

The other possibility is that being fed frustrates and annoys your baby. She gets cross at the way the spoon comes too quickly, or not quickly enough…not like being at the breast or on the bottle where she is more in control. Babies like this often change once they're able to feed themselves a little, which can happen from about five months onwards.

There's so rarely any need to worry about a baby who is taking less solid food than you think she 'ought' to have. As long as your baby is having milk, continuing to maintain a good weight, and staying healthy, there is no rush. Ask your health visitor's advice if your baby gets beyond six or seven months without appearing to show much interest in other foods, just to check everything's okay.

All babies go through occasional days when they don't seem particularly hungry. Like adults, their appetites vary from time to time.

YOUR QUESTIONS ANSWERED

Does my baby need vitamin drops at five months? I've heard conflicting opinions on this topic.

You're right: there are differing ideas on whether babies actually need vitamin drops or not. The drops, by the way, contain Vitamins A, C and D in a pleasant-tasting fluid, given with a tiny dropper direct into the baby's mouth.

Current guidelines recommend daily vitamin drops from the age of six months to five years, and acknowledge a case for giving drops from the age of a month. The drops are a safeguard, to protect a baby or child through times of illness or faddiness, when food intake may not be adequate. The drops themselves, when given in the recommended dose, are entirely harmless, of course, even when given to babies who don't actually need them. If you're confident your baby is healthy and well-fed, and she gets outside regularly (the body can manufacture Vitamin D from sunlight) then she probably doesn't need any supplementary vitamins. If she's been poorly, or if she doesn't feed very well, then they may be needed. Ask your health visitor for advice. Remember that some babies do develop fussy eating habits as they get older, and you may want to offer drops then, even temporarily.

You can get vitamin drops at most child health clinics. You may be able to get them free of charge.

I worry because my baby doesn't seem to want anything to drink with her meals. She has breakfast, lunch and tea, but quite often takes no fluid at all, though she is offered a cup every time. She breastfeeds three or four times a day. Might she become thirsty?

If she does get thirsty, she'll take a drink from the cup you offer her, or simply spend more time on the breast. Healthy babies don't allow themselves to go short of any necessary fluids. Just carry on what you're doing, making sure there is a drink for her should she want it. Don't ever try to force her to drink. It seems odd, but some babies are definitely more thirsty than others. You'll probably find she gradually comes round to using a cup as she gets older and more active, or in warmer weather.

I know you're supposed to go gradually with solid foods, and to build up from a slow start, but my four-month-old son is a guzzler! He absolutely adores food, and he's already on three full meals a day, plus four 200 ml bottles of formula. I honestly haven't forced the pace – I've followed his lead.

Don't worry. As long as you are doing what your son seems to want and enjoy, and you're not filling him up with sweetened puddings, or sugary rusks and biscuits, then it's highly likely your son's appetite reflects his nutritional needs at the moment. You could start offering him finger foods, if you like (see p. 72) – he'll probably really enjoy exploring food in this way. The more independent he is about feeding, the less you'll have to worry about whether you're giving him too much or not.

I'd always thought I'd breastfeed my baby for about a year, but already at six months she's starting to reject it. She turns her head away when I offer her the breast, and for the past two days she's only accepted a feed in the evening. Could she be weaning herself away from it? She has three meals a day, plus drinks of fruit juice or water.

It's possible you're daughter is coming off the breast of her own accord. This can happen with a baby as young as this, although it's quite unusual. It's more likely to happen if the mother has taken steps to cut down on the breastfeeds for whatever reason, which reduces the baby's dependency on breast milk. It could also be that your daughter is teething, and finds it uncomfortable to feed, or simply that she's going through an inexplicable phase that could be quite short-lived. A breastfeeding counsellor would be able to suggest other possibilities, and to help you work out what you want to do in response.

You may want to hang on in there, continuing to offer the breast, so your daughter knows you're still available if she does come back to feeding more often. On the other hand, you may decide to wean your daughter from the breast completely, or to keep up the evening feed for as long as you both want, and forget about offering the breast at other times.

It's likely, by the way, that your milk will return quickly to its previous quantity if you go back to feeding more frequently. Mothers who've been feeding for several months find they can keep up a supply on very little stimulation.

My mother says she and her friends used to put cereals and even other foods directly into the baby's bottle. Why isn't this done so much now?

This means of feeding can cause choking, as the baby sucks in a mouthful of thick food, which then 'goes down the wrong way'. The other reason why it isn't recommended is because it teaches the baby very little about different tastes, textures, or about chewing. If everything comes through the bottle teat in the same smooth sort of way, feeding ceases to be an enjoyable, sociable, learning experience.

My health visitor says babies should have cereal no more than once a day. Why is this? Is it harmful to have too much of it?

It's not actually harmful, and it wouldn't hurt a young baby just starting on solids to have a small amount of cereal more than once a day, but the concern is that too much cereal fills a baby up, so there's no room for an introduction to a growing range of other foods from different food groups (such as fruits and vegetables). The balance of the diet is then tipped too far towards the carbohydrates. Once your baby is really joining in with family meals, and having the occasional snack as well, it would be surprising if she doesn't have cereal, in one form or another (e.g. bread, pasta, rice), twice or more every day as a routine. After all, she may have bread in the form of toast for breakfast, pasta or rice with her lunch, and then bread again at tea time.

How can I get my baby to enjoy savoury foods? She's five months old and refuses vegetables in favour of chocolate puddings!

It's natural for humans, especially baby humans, to have a sweet tooth; after all, breast milk itself is naturally sweet. There are, however, good reasons for making sure your baby doesn't get 'hooked' on filling up with sweetened foods to the exclusion of other foods. Your baby's still easily young enough to have her tastes changed, so don't worry.

Your baby may like sweet vegetables such as carrots and parsnips, and most babies like mashed potato. Make the savoury food look as good as the sweet stuff – even young babies respond to that. Try her with banana, pears or dessert apple. If you stop giving her puds, she will forget about them. Don't have them in the house, so you avoid the temptation of giving in to her, when she refuses her dinner and you feel she 'must' have something. Then, as she gets older, keep sweetened puddings for special occasions and treats.

5 A healthy diet for your child

You'll help your child get off to a good start in life by trying to ensure she eats the right sort of food. Poor nutrition can affect your child's growth, development and health, and it can also increase the risk of illness in adulthood.

This long-lasting effect may be because eating an unhealthy diet in the early years reflect poor eating habits in the family as a whole, and so the child grows up into adulthood still eating an unhealthy diet; or it may be because a poor diet in babyhood and early childhood has a direct effect on the way the body manages disease years later.

Nutritionists are still learning about the elements of a healthy diet, and the effects of a poor one. The essential nutrients in anyone's diet, whatever their age, are carbohydrates (including fibre, starches and sugars) fats (including essential fatty acids), proteins, vitamins, minerals and water.

Toddlers and young children need the same elements as adults. They need a lot of dietary energy — calories — relative to their size. They can't take a great deal of food in at any single meal, which is why they prefer small meals with snacks in between. Fat is more important in their diet than in adults', not just because of the calories, but because of the extra vitamins in it.

An ideal diet for a child aged one year or over (up to about five years) will have some meat (red and white) and fish, whole milk, eggs, dairy products like cheeses, fromage frais and yoghurt, vegetables, fruit, bread and other cereals like rice, pasta, wheat and oat-based breakfast cereals. Vegetarian children will need other sources of protein, like pulses and soya.

Most young children have most of these foods fairly regularly. If you find your child really doesn't like, say, vegetables, you can offer them in a different form. Try vegetable soup, for example, or serve them raw as finger foods, with a 'dip'. As long as your child has enough food to satisfy her appetite, her diet is based on a range of mainly fresh foods of different types, and she's developing and growing, with lots of energy, you can be confident you're doing fine as a parent.

A suggested menu of day's meals for babies and children from six months up to three years is given below. The ideas reflect what children in these age groups generally enjoy, and they'll all give a healthy balance of nutrients. Exact quantities aren't given, or timings. These will depend on your child's appetite, plus the routine that suits her, and the rest of your household.

A day's menu

At 6 to 12 months

On waking:	milk feed
Breakfast:	fingers of toast with polyunsaturated spread; porridge, made from oats or baby rice
Mid-morning:	drink of diluted fruit juice from a cup
Lunch:	mashed potato, topped with a small mount of grated, melted cheese; milk feed
Mid-afternoon:	drink from a cup
Tea:	yoghurt; small banana sandwich; milk feed
Evening:	milk feed

At 12 months to 2 years:
By this age children should be eating pretty much the same as the rest of the family.

On waking:	drink of milk
Breakfast:	boiled egg, with toast with polyunsaturated spread. Drink of milk
Mid-morning:	drink of juice, half an apple, peeled and sliced
Lunch:	thick vegetable soup, with bread and polyunsaturated spread; fromage frais; milk
Mid-afternoon:	drink of juice, rusk or bread crust
Tea:	pasta with tuna fish or sausage and peas, satsuma; milk
Evening:	milk

At 2 to 3 years:
Breakfast: cereal with milk; toast with polyunsaturated spread and yeast spread
Mid-morning: drink of juice, banana
Lunch: fish pie with tomato, baked beans; yoghurt; drink of juice
Mid-afternoon: drink of juice, slice bread and polyunsaturated spread
Tea: scrambled egg on toast, with small green salad; dessert pear, mashed

Note: as these menus suggest, children tend not to need a drink on waking as they get older, and they are less likely to wake at a very early hour like 6.00, or if they do, they may not demand attention. Evening drinks tend to fade away as the months go on, but if you like this way of marking bedtime, and many families do, then carry on. Try to stick to milk or water as commercially-prepared bedtime drinks are usually sweetened and can damage your child's teeth if given last thing at night.

MILK

What sort?

For the first year of life, your baby is best off on breast or formula milk. Small quantities of whole pasteurised milk (that is, milkman's milk or 'doorstep milk'; whole milk is sold with a silver top) can be used in cooking from six months.

After the age of 12 months, continue with breast milk or formula if you like. You can also give whole milk as a drink. The reason why whole milk isn't recommended until then is because it is relatively low in iron and some vitamins and high in sodium.

If your child is a very good eater, you can give her semi-skimmed milk as a drink (this is sold with a red striped top) from the age of 2 years. It has half the fat of whole milk, and also less of the fat-soluble vitamins A and D. For this reason, average or faddy eaters should continue with whole milk until they are nearer to 5 years. (Skimmed milk should only be given after 5 years.)

A pint of milk a day?

A pint of milk a day is probably too much for many toddlers. Your child needs to learn to rely on solid food for her nutrients. The nutrients in milk are a handy top-up but increasingly should not provide the main item in ensuring that your child is well fed.

Milk is a very useful source of minerals such as calcium, protein, some vitamins and fat; it's relatively cheap and widely available. So it has quite a lot going for it, if your child likes it. If your family aims to have a low-fat diet in general, then giving your children whole milk is a good way of making sure they have the comparatively higher-fat diet they need. If you offer your child whole milk in food or as a drink two or three times a day. and supplement her 'dairy' intake with cheeses, baby yoghurt and fromage frais, you won't go far wrong.

Some children just don't like milk, or they don't like it in this quantity. A few actually can't take any cow's milk at all, because of allergy or intolerance.

If your child has a milk allergy (see p. 64) or simply doesn't like it, you'll need to take advice to ensure she gets what she needs from elsewhere in her diet.

SUGAR AND YOUR CHILD

Many foods contain sugars in a natural form, and sugar may be added in small amounts to other foods to make them palatable.

Sugar is sometimes seen as a demon food, and a few parents are prepared to avoid it completely when feeding their babies and children. In fact, avoiding sugar totally, in all its forms, is neither possible nor desirable, but there are good reasons for avoiding having added sugar too often because of the effect it can have on teeth.

Sugar is harmful to teeth in two ways, which reinforce each other's effect: it tends to make food sticky, which means it stays on the teeth for longer after eating; and it acts on plaque (the film of debris on the teeth and gums), feeding the bacteria in it. This produces acids which attack the teeth, eating away at the protective enamel and, eventually, causing the rotting-away we know of as tooth decay, and which dentists call dental caries. It also contributes to gum disease.

It's up to you how far you take this, of course. Some parents ban all cakes, sweets, biscuits, sweetened drinks and chocolate for ever; others keep them as very occasional treats. You must make sure your baby's diet is not greatly limited by this approach because she simply refuses to eat enough unsweetened foods.

Others try quite hard to resist for the first years of their children's lives, and then find they have to relax their ideas as their children meet outside influences at playgroup, parties and at relatives' houses.

There is absolutely no doubt that sugar leads directly to poor dental health, and as we don't actually need added sugar in our diet, why not cut it out altogether?

However, food is more than merely feeding our bodies. Food is enjoyable, and a means of sharing experience with others. Sweets, and sweetened foods, are a fun treat that most of us like. In moderation, and with care paid to dental health, a total ban on all sweetened foods should not be necessary.

Here are some guidelines, for you to adopt or adapt according to how strongly you feel.

- If you bottle feed, don't let your child stay asleep with a bottle in her mouth. Apart from the risk of choking, anything except plain water will bathe her teeth in sugar.

- Avoid letting your toddler swig from a feeding bottle for much of the day – a possibility if your child has bottles after about a year. Feeding bottles used in this way mean the teeth are again bathed in sugar, and cause the phenomenon known to dentists as 'nursing bottle caries', where the front teeth are decayed and rotten before the age of two. Cups are in any case better for teeth, and don't get lugged around as a comforter.

○ Choose low-sugar rusks or sugar-free rusks, or avoid them and give bread crusts instead.

○ Don't always give biscuits as a snack. Choose pieces of fruit as a regular alternative. If biscuits are served at the playgroup or toddler group, suggest fruit instead.

○ Always dilute fruit juices with plenty of water.

○ Keep chocolates and sweets as an occasional treat for as long as you can, or once your child starts to understand about the different days of the week, you can have them on one particular day each week.

○ Always make sure your child's teeth are brushed well, every morning and every evening before she goes to bed. You will have to do it for her, or at least finish off the job properly, for some time (I'd say until about 5 years and even older if you think she might miss bits).

○ Remember frequent sugar consumption causes damage, more than actual quantity. A packet of sweets eaten straight away causes less harm than several sweets eaten across the whole day.

○ Don't buy very sweet breakfast cereals, or sweetened bedtime drinks, and don't add sugar to anything unless you have to for the sake of taste.

○ Read the labels of foods you buy and choose the ones with the least sugar in them.

○ Don't feel you need to offer a pudding at meal times. Encourage your child to grow up expecting a piece of fruit as the finishing touch to her dinner (means less work for you, anyway).

○ Start visiting the dentist regularly with your child from the age of two years.

What about a 'sweet tooth'?

Experts have found no good evidence for supporting the idea that giving sweet foods to a baby means she'll develop a 'sweet tooth' – meaning she's hooked on sweetened stuff forever. It's actually natural for humans to prefer sweet to sour. Breast milk is sweet, for example. It's thought that in evolutionary terms, humans developed a taste for sweetness as a way of protecting themselves against harmful fruits and other foods. In the main, if a food tastes sweet, it's probably okay to eat, that is, it won't poison you, or give you a bad stomach ache. If it's bitter, it is probably not advisable to eat it.

So while it's a good idea to make sure your child learns to enjoy a wide range of savoury foods, there's probably very little you can do to stop her actually enjoying sweets and other sugary foods.

WHAT ABOUT ADDITIVES?

Most commercially packaged baby food is free of artificial preservatives, flavourings and colourings, known as 'additives'. This doesn't mean it's the same as your own home-cooked food (see p. 46), but it does mean your baby is protected from any adverse reaction to artificial ingredients. Baby food may have natural additives that would not be part of the food in its 'normal' state. For instance, strawberry-flavoured foods may have added strawberry flavouring, and red vegetable colouring.

Additives are present in many of the other processed foods available today. They are there to improve flavour, or to make the food last longer before going 'off' or to maintain its colour and texture, or to aid in the processing itself, for instance to help a cake mix rise on baking.

A few people are sensitive to certain additives, but for most of us, additives are considered to be safe as long as they have under-gone acceptance by a series of advisory and safety committees of the European Community. The ones that have been approved are given a coding, called an E number, and they are permitted in certain foods. Sometimes, a previously permitted additive is withdrawn from the approved list and new ones are added.

Additives have been implicated in some cases of hyperactivity (see below); colourants, particularly tartrazine (E102), which is used to colour foods and drinks orange, have been linked with behavioural problems. Many studies have either rejected the link, or been unable to establish it, however. Nevertheless, it's reasonably easy to avoid colourants if you feel your child suffers behavioural disturbances after eating or drinking something with them in.

If you prefer to base your family's diet on more natural and unprocessed foods, you can avoid additives by checking the labels of processed foods and avoiding the ones with long lists of E numbers or named additives. Processed food without additives is likely to be closer to its natural state, however, remember canning, smoking, freezing or heating are very common processes in food manufacture, involving no additives, and they too can take the food you buy away from a totally natural state.

Fresh food, unprocessed and prepared soon after purchase is likely to retain more of its quality and nutritional benefits than anything you buy that's been through a manufacturing process (with the exception of frozen vegetables), and it is likely to be cheaper, and possibly tastier, too. In particular, the vitamin content of many foods may be affected by processing. Additives do, however, allow us to have a wider range of foods, and they have a role to play in today's diets.

HYGIENE, SAFETY AND FOOD

When your baby's young, she is more susceptible to food poisoning – the blanket term for any disease caused by food or drink that's harmful – either because the food or drink has changed because it's no longer fresh, or because it has been contaminated by coming into contact with something harmful. As your baby grows, her immune system becomes more mature and able to fight off possible food poisoning. Even so, common-sense rules about buying, storing and handling food are important for all members of your household. Babies and young children under two years of age, along with pregnant women, are considered to be in one of the 'at risk' groups of people more likely to suffer ill effects from food poisoning.

When choosing food for children under two, the Food Safety Advisory Centre recommends you avoid:

○ unpasteurised milk ('green top') and products made from unpasteurised milk.

○ soft, mould-ripened cheeses (for example, Brie, Camembert, Danish Blue).

○ soft whip ice cream from machines.

When preparing food for anyone, and especially your child:

○ Wash your hands before preparing food.

○ Wash all fruit and vegetables, including ready-prepared salad vegetables.

○ Keep animals out of the kitchen.

○ Keep chopping boards clean by scrubbing with detergent.

○ Keep your fridge at the correct temperature (5°C or lower).

○ Store left-overs in the fridge, covered.

○ Store meat in the fridge: keep cooked and raw meats separate, away from other foods, and well covered.

○ Cook food thoroughly.

○ Defrost frozen food thoroughly.

○ Check 'use by' dates and don't use once passed.

○ Don't reheat food more than once.

○ Don't keep food in opened cans.

- ○ pâté sold from the delicatessen counter; canned and jarred pâté is okay, as long as it's stored in the fridge once opened and eaten within two days.

- ○ cook-chill food such as cold, ready-roasted poultry, ready-meals from shops.

- ○ raw and lightly cooked eggs (scrambled is okay, as long as they are firm).

You can get more information by contacting Foodline, the freephone advice line of the Food Safety Advisory Centre (see p. 98).

YOUR CHILD WITH SPECIAL DIETARY NEEDS

Not all children need exactly the same sort of foods to stay healthy; a few have health problems connected with food, or made worse by the 'wrong' foods, or else they need a special diet in order to stay healthy, because of problems with metabolism (the way they process certain foods).

You'll need more information than this book can give you if your own baby or child has problems of this sort, but here's a quick run-down of some diet-related syndromes, and a brief explanation of each.

Failure to thrive

This is a description, rather than a diagnosis. If a baby or child fails to gain weight over time, or gains weight only very slowly or starts to lose it, then further investigations are needed to establish the cause. There may be a physical reason, for example some babies with a heart problem fail to gain weight properly. But usually the cause is dietary, that is, that the child is not getting enough of the nutrients needed for growth.

There are different reasons for this. It may be that breastfeeding is providing very little intake. Or that the child has a medical condition like Down's syndrome, which makes it diffcult to suck. Or that the older child is a faddy eater. Sometimes, the difficulty lies with the family's social or emotional circumstances. Some parents need help and information about the amount and type of food their baby needs. Health workers became concerned in recent years about something termed the 'muesli-belt syndrome'. Apparently, noticeable numbers of middle-class parents were feeding their toddlers on low-fat, high-fibre diets, in the mistaken belief that this was healthy for them. Instead, it caused poor weight gain and diarrhoea. It also appears that some parents for whatever reason, don't notice when their children are hungry, and the children learn from an early age not to make demands for food.

In many failure-to-thrive situations, there's no real cause for concern in the longer term, and the baby or child has a period of 'catch up growth' without further problems.

Metabolism problems

About 1500 babies are born each year with a metabolic disorder – a condition meaning the child can't process food properly –that can be helped by a special diet.

Phenylketonuria (PKU)
All new babies are screened for this towards the end of the first week of life, when a tiny sample of blood is taken, usually from the heel (this test is known as the Guthrie test) and sent for checking. A baby who turns out to have PKU (and the rate is less than 1 in every 10,000, or just 60 babies a year in the whole of the UK) is deficient in an important enzyme necessary to digest protein. A special low-protein diet is then devised for her, according to the severity of the condition.

Hyperlipidaemia
A disorder that predisposes to early heart attack, because of an abnormally raised cholesterol level, resulting from an inability to digest fats. It is more common in children from families with a history of early onset heart disease. Children with this sort of background will be screened, and given a special diet to overcome the problem.

Cystic fibrosis

As well as causing lung problems, cystic fibrosis also affects the pancreas. This part of the digestive system helps to ensure that the nutrients are absorbed from the gut. Drugs are available which can make up for this failure in the function of the pancreas.

Other disorders include *galactosaemia,* which is an inability to digest the milk sugar lactose, dealt with by a milk-free diet.

Food intolerance

This is a reaction by the body to a food or foods. The body appears to 'reject' the food by becoming sick or by developing other symptoms.

Technically, a food allergy is different from food intolerance, because an allergy implies that the body's immune system is involved in producing antibodies to the food in order to fight it. With food intolerance, the harmful effect doesn't involve the immune system.

You can decrease the chances of your child developing food intolerance and/or allergy by:

o **breastfeeding exclusively for at least three months (some authorities recommend longer – four to six months).**

o **avoiding the introduction of eggs and gluten-containing foods until your baby is five to six months old.**

Sensitisation is the first stage of allergy – once you are sensitised to a substance, you may produce symptoms when you next come across it. Eggs and gluten are known to be common allergens, and a very young baby is more likely to become sensitised to them than an older one, whose immune system is better developed.

The most common forms of food intolerance are listed below.

Cow's milk protein intolerance

This may become obvious in early babyhood in bottle-fed babies. In severe cases, the baby fails to thrive, and suffers from sickness and diarrhoea. The treatment is usually to give a formula without any cow's milk in it, soya or other specially-made formula. Mothers in this situation could consider relactating, as breast milk doesn't produce this problem. Relactating, (bringing back the breast milk supply), is not always easy, however, and babies used to the sucking action they use on the teat may not know what to do with a nipple.

Some babies don't show signs of cow's milk protein intolerance until later. This intolerance may be linked with eczema, or asthma, thought to be an allergic reaction in many cases.

Breastfed babies won't demonstrate cow's milk protein intolerance until weaning age, although some studies have suggested that a few breastfed babies may develop allergies or intolerance to the minute traces of cow's milk protein in their mother's breast milk. It's thought that a colicky baby – one who cries for a long time, and appears in pain or discomfort without having any disease or illness to explain it – may be helped if the mother cuts out all dairy products from her diet. However, babies almost always grow out of colicky behaviour whatever you do. It would be very difficult to 'prove' that your dairy-free diet made the difference. Even if the crying starts again if you reintroduce milk, you couldn't be sure your baby wasn't crying for another reason. However, colic is a miserable phenomenon for all the family, especially, presumably, for the baby, so a few dairy-free days have got to be worth a try. If you stick with a dairy-free diet, you'll need to ensure you make up any gaps in your diet from other foods.

There's no evidence that other animal's milk, such as goat's or sheep's, is any less likely to produce a reaction, and there's no reason to think that these milks are 'healthier' for babies in any way. Goat's and sheep's milk are low in some vitamins. Some may be unpasturised and so could contain germs causing disease such as brucellosis.

Hyperactivity
There is some evidence that this condition may be related to an intolerance to some foods, at least in some cases. Hyperactive

children are more than just energetic or 'difficult'; they are often sleepless as well, and hard to control.

Some parents have found that if they make sure their child follows a special diet, there is an all-round improvement in the situation. It takes some commitment and patience to stick to the diet, which may take time to work at first. It is important to have expert guidance from a dietitian specialised in advising about young children, or such diets may be nutritionallly inadequate. Sceptics say it is the increased attention that improves the behaviour, and that the difference the food itself makes is an illusion. However, it's worth a try if you feel nothing else has helped with your child's behaviour.

Coeliac disease
This is a condition that affects the lining of the small intestine, which prevents the body from tolerating gluten, the protein in wheat and some other cereals. It is less common than it used to be even 20 or 30 years ago, probably because parents now delay the introduction of wheat cereal to their babies. Early introduction of gluten can damage the intestine lining. It's also thought that colostrum – the early milk made by the breasts – protects the gut from harm. Since the 1970s, a higher proportion of babies have received colostrum, compared to the previous generation, and the first cereal recommended for babies is usually rice, which is gluten-free.

Coeliac disease shows itself in a failure to thrive, and pale, bulky stools, and possibly constipation. It may not show up until toddlerhood. Treatment is a gluten-free diet, usually for life.

If you discover your child needs to be on a special diet, you'll need help. Ask your community dietitian for recipes, and sources of manufactured foods. It's not a good to idea to radically change your child's diet without this sort of professional back-up, anyway.

You'll also need support if it's decided to put your child on an exclusion diet, which is sometimes done to establish any possible food links with symptoms. It works by restricting your child to a very few food items for a short time, say a fortnight, while you notice any change in symptoms. Then, item by item, foods are restored to her diet, until you come across the one that causes the problem.

It's important that you don't try to put your child on an exclusion diet yourself; your child may need supplements to plug the nutritional gaps while building up to a full diet once again. For example, most exclusion diets omit milk as a likely culprit in a case of food intolerance. Your dietitian or doctor may prescribe vitamin and mineral supplements for your child to take in the meantime, and will make sure your child is getting enough calcium from other sources.

Many dietary problems have their own self-help groups of parents who can swap tips, and offer mutual support.

WHAT HAPPENS IF MY CHILD IS ILL?

The most common minor illness in babies and children is a bout of sickness and diarrhoea. Ask your doctor's advice, especially with a very young baby, who can become dehydrated very quickly in these circumstances, and very poorly.

If your child doesn't need any actual treatment (bar the rehydration mixture your doctor may prescribe), then you may wonder whether to keep her food intake up.

With a toddler, be guided by her appetite, but keep up fluid levels with diluted fruit juice. A baby or toddler who is breastfed can have breast milk ad lib, as breast milk has good anti-diarrhoeal and anti-infective properties, and will speed recovery.

If your baby is wholly or mainly bottle fed, you may be advised to give 'half-strength feeds', which means the feed is diluted with twice the usual volume of water. Always check with your doctor before doing this, however, as it may not be necessary.

YOUR QUESTIONS ANSWERED

My two-year-old son really doesn't like milk. He doesn't have an allergy, as he has some milk every day on cereal, and never reacts to it. But how can I get him to drink it from a cup?
You might not manage to do so, if he has a strong dislike to milk. However, milk is important becasue it provides calcium which is needed for growing bones. Continue giving him milk on cereal and in other foods, and make sure he has whole milk yoghurt, cheese and fromage frais. Check with your health visitor; it's likely that once you take into account the rest of his diet, he is getting everything he needs, despite a low milk intake.

How can I tell if my child is allergic to any foods?
Don't make this sort of firm diagnosis yourself. If you suspect a food or food type of causing an allergy, speak to your health visitor or GP. They may refer you to a paediatrician or a dietitian who can carry out a test. Then, you may need help in working out a healthy diet without this food

6 Your older baby – six months to one year

At six months some babies are still in the very early stages of mixed feeding. Others may be enjoying a widening range of solid foods. She may be eating two or three solid meals a day, plus drinks between meals and maybe the occasional snack of a rusk, or a piece of bread or fruit. Some babies are still in the very early stages of mixed feeding, and that's fine, too.

Most babies are now able to sit in a high chair, or in a special chair that slides on to the table (make sure your baby is well-strapped in to whatever seat you have her in). This makes it a lot easier for her to join in with your meals.

A sheet, old curtain or mat underneath your baby's chair is useful for catching crumbs and other mess. Check, too, when you're buying a high chair, that the tray comes off for easy cleaning.

Sociable, happy mealtimes make it easier for your baby to make the transition from 'baby foods' to family foods. she can see what you're eating, and enjoy the fact that she's having the same.

Aim to adjust the times of your baby's meals to your own. For example, a baby who's been having a small amount of solid food with a bottle or breastfeed at about 11.00 can be encouraged to wait until lunchtime. A drink from a cup, or a rusk, will keep her going until then.

You too may need to change the time you eat, to accommodate her, for a while, anyway. Some babies in the second half of the first year need an afternoon sleep, and they start flagging at about midday. Leave lunch too late and they'll drop off to sleep actually sitting there in the high chair while you wave a spoon temptingly under her nose.

If you can get your baby's lunch inside her before she goes to sleep, it makes life simpler. She may sleep for longer, and of course it means you're not having to give her lunch when she does wake up. This might mean getting something organised by about 11.30.

For many families, eating tea at 5.00 or 5.30, which is when most young babies and toddlers are ready for theirs, doesn't fit with other circumstances, such as the time you and/or your partner get in from a day's work. You may prefer an evening meal rather later.

If you can, have a snack with your baby at about this time, or else give your baby a snack, and then all eat together.

Different families will work out different routines, and they may change from day to day, or at the weekends. The main points to remember are that your baby will prefer eating with someone else who enjoys her company, at least some of the time, and that as she grows older, she can have more and more 'ordinary' food, that is her need for special provision at the table grows smaller.

WHAT CAN MY BABY EAT?

At some time around six months your baby can have just about anything.

You can now give:

o   meat.

o   wheat-based foods, eg family breakfast cereals, and breads.

o   small amounts of cow's milk (whole pasteurised milk) in cooking.

o   other dairy products, such as yoghurt, fromage frais, soft cheese, such as soft cheese spread; hard cheese is fine, too, though it's easier for your baby to eat if it's grated and melted first.

o   you can start giving your baby egg – at first, it should only be the well-cooked yolk and when you're sure she can tolerate that without a problem, you can give the whole egg, white as well. All eggs should be hardboiled.

○ oranges and other citrus fruits are suitable, now, but avoid whole nuts until after your baby is 5 years old; finely ground nuts used in cooking, and smooth peanut butter, are perfectly acceptable, and a useful source of protein, especially for vegetarian and vegan babies.

Mix and match

At this stage, you can combine lots of textures and flavours, adding rice, bread, pasta or potato, and a little protein in the form of hard boiled egg (yolk only at first), fish, meat, poultry, dairy produce or pulses.

Start with something simple like adding one or two teaspoons of grated cheddar or edam cheese or a mashed hard-boiled egg

What to avoid

○ Fried, fatty foods could upset your baby's tummy if they're given in large quantities.

○ Be careful, too, about salty foods.

○ Don't add salt to your baby's foods, and if you add salt to your own food, remove your baby's portion before you add it.

yolk to a tablespoon of well-mashed potato, yam or cauliflower. Moisten with a little milk (breast, formula or cow's).

MANUFACTURED BABY FOODS FOR YOUR CHILD

There are bound to be times, throughout this second six months and beyond, when it's convenient to give your baby something out of a jar or packet.

The same advantages and dis-

'I find I give packets and jars less and less as my daughter gets older. I've found that now she eats a variety of foods, there's always something I can give her that's quick and easy when time is short. She likes mashed banana mixed with yoghurt at the moment, and that's just as easy as opening a can.'

advantages described on p. 45 apply; in particular, babies over six months can cope with different textures quite readily. Manufacturers have cottoned on to this, of course, and label some of their foods with names like 'stage 2' or 'junior', and there are plenty of lumpy bits in them.

Again, don't swallow the implication of the ads that your baby has to have commercial foods in order to be well fed. Now that she can have more or less the same as you, you should feel free to use the packets and jars when you aren't eating, or when you have nothing else suitable, or when there just isn't time for anything more complicated. See the recipe section for ideas you can all share (p. 86).

Presenting food

Don't bother blending or puréeing especially for your baby. Help her get used to the fact that foods come in all degrees of lumpiness and smoothness. But use your judgement: you may need to blend hard pieces of meat, for example.

FINGER FOODS

This is the term used to describe foods your baby can feed herself with, without the need to wield a spoon or fork.

Most babies like the chance to feed themselves, and it makes things easier for you, too. Put the food direct on to your baby's high chair tray, or on a plate on the tray. Obviously, you'll choose items that are easy to handle, and which aren't too messy. A few babies dislike handling foods that are too sticky and sloppy, anyway.

Always stay with your baby when she's feeding herself. She may choke, and need your help in getting the food out of her mouth.

Teething tip

Freeze sticks of carrot, celery and cucumber. Let your baby gnaw on them when she's teething to soothe sore gums.

Some perfect finger foods:

o   slices of peeled, cored, eating apple.

o   sticks of carrot, celery (stringy bits peeled off), cucumber (seeds removed for young babies).

o   tiny sandwiches with a scraping of butter or sunflower spread, and marmite; peanut butter; grated cheese and skinned, de-seeded tomato; cottage cheese; tahini; no-sugar fruit spreads; mashed banana.

o   fingers of nan, pitta or chappati.

o   crackers or savoury cheese biscuits (no salt versions).

o   buttered or marmite toast soldiers.

o   fingers of cheese on toast or pizza.

o   cubes of cheese.

o   peas (cooked).

o   boiled potato, chopped.

o   pasta shapes.

o   fingers of cooked vegetable.

o   rice cakes (from health shops), with or without a spread.

o   bread crusts, baked in a slow oven, as rusks.

ADAPTING THE FAMILY MEAL

When your baby joins in with the family for most or all of her meals, you will still need to mash or chop her food. Keep it moist with gravy, a sauce or cooking juices. Most main meals can be adapted for a baby or toddler. The only cooking methods that aren't suitable are deep-frying or roasting with a lot of fat, but an occasional small amount will be fine.

Casseroles, stews, grills, hotpots, roasts (without much fat), pasta and rice dishes are for everyone. Simply cook the recipe in the normal way but without salt or strong flavourings. When the dish is cooked, take out the baby's portion and finish seasoning the remainder for everyone else.

USING EQUIPMENT

Learning about spoons

Most babies of under a year won't manage to use a spoon or a fork very efficiently, but they can certainly start to learn.

When you spoonfeed your baby, give her a spoon as well. She'll soon start to copy you, putting her spoon in the food and trying to get food up with it. There'll be times when it all starts being too much fun, and she'll use the spoon for chucking the food about, and deliberately putting it anywhere but her mouth. Don't get too cross – it's all part of learning, after all! Simply take the spoon, or the food away, and explain why you're doing so.

Shallow baby dishes and plates are helpful. You can get plates which stick to the tray with a suction pad. They may work for you, but I've seen them act as a temptation to a curious baby. She has to try and get it off that tray, and when she manages to do so, it springs off very suddenly, with messy results.

Most toddlers won't manage a fork until after they've mastered a spoon. Knives and cutting skills come much later.

Drinks from a cup

By now, your baby has probably had a few tries at drinking from a cup. You don't have to use the special baby cups with a lid and a spout, though these are usually easier for a baby to handle by herself than normal ones. A few babies prefer to sip or lap from a normal

'I have two children, and they've both been very different. My elder son has always wanted a lot to drink – at least a cup of juice every mealtime, plus three or four drinks of water, juice or milk between meals. The younger one has never seemed anything like as thirsty. He sometimes has a drink with a meal, and sometimes not. He hardly ever has a drink between meals.'

cup, however, held by you at first. Then, as they get older, they can hold it and tip it themselves.

Have a cup where your baby can reach it when she's eating her meal. It doesn't matter if she doesn't have a drink from it. Some babies don't seem to get very thirsty.

Offer a drink mid-morning and mid-afternoon. If you want to finish breastfeeding or bottle feeding, give her a cup instead of the usual feed (for more information on weaning from breast or bottle, see p. 35).

FOLLOW-ON MILK: A BETTER ALTERNATIVE?

Follow-on milks are branded formula milks, marketed as an alternative to cow's milk (doorstep) for babies over six months of age. They are higher in iron than cow's milk. However, two perfectly adequate alternatives already exist, suitable for babies of this age and older – namely breast milk and ordinary formula. There is no reason to change to a follow-on milk.

Follow-on milk may be a healthier alternative to ordinary milk in the 6–12 month age range. There is some evidence that mothers see the six month stage as a time of change, when they feel they want to mark the fact that the baby is growing up, and eating and drinking differently. The manufacturers claim they can mark the change by switching to follow-on.

It's up to you what you do, but remember there's no real nutritional reason for change.

A WORD ON IRON

By six months, the iron stores your baby was born with need replenishing from her diet, which is why it's advisable for her to be making some progress with solids by now. If you are breastfeeding and your baby is not getting any solid foods at six months she may run a risk of iron-deficiency, and occasionally of anaemia.

If your baby has shown very little interest in anything but milk, she probably will very shortly. Just make it easy for her by sitting her in a high chair or on your lap at mealtimes, and offering her samples of different foods.

If this doesn't help. and your baby gets beyond six months still actively refusing all solid food, then ask your health visitor for advice. She may have ideas on how to get your baby more interested, and check that her health and development is okay.

YOUR QUESTIONS ANSWERED

We're vegetarians, and we often have lentils and other pulses. When can I start giving my baby these foods?

From about five or six months old. Cook them well, and mash them. If they turn out a bit dry and hard to spoon-feed, you can moisten them with apple juice, which gives a pleasant flavour most babies like. It's important to make sure your baby gets enough calories. Too much bulky food will make it difficult to get enough food to provide the calories needed for growth and development.

Infants and young children being weaned on a vegetarian diet particularly need vitamin C. Try a dilute drink of orange juice at most meals.

Of course vegetarian babies are just as healthy as meat-eaters. World-wide, many children are vegetarian and never eat meat, for cultural or religious reasons. However, it may be helpful to get specialised information about weaning on to a vegetarian diet from an organisation like the Vegetarian Society, especially if you are a 'new' vegetarian.

What about vegan babies?

You need to take extra care if you intend weaning your baby on to a vegan diet, which avoids all animal products, including dairy foods and eggs. The main nutrient a weaned baby might go short of is vitamin B12. It's recommended that vegan babies are breastfed for a long time, at least until into the second year and beyond, if possible. Then, a soya formula fortified with B12 can be used as a drink and in cooking. The Vegan Society can help with lots of information.

I'm sure my baby has developed a sweet tooth. She loves fruit puddings and sweetened desserts, but rejects the savoury food I make her. Can I change her tastes?

It's natural for babies, and indeed all human beings, to enjoy sweet foods, but you're right to be anxious about your daughter eating sweetened foods instead of other foods.

You can't make her dislike sweet stuff, but you can help her extend her range of foods that she likes. Give her fresh fruit instead of puddings for dessert, and make sure the vegetables and savouries you offer are attractive to look at, and easy for her to eat with her fingers. Try her with some of the naturally sweet vegetables, like carrots, parsnips and blanched green peppers. If she doesn't want much savoury food, assume she's not hungry, rather than moving straight on to the sweet course.

My son is nine months, and he still wakes up in the night, maybe three or four times. He can't seem to get back to sleep unless he has a drink of warmed milk. He eats well during the day. Can he really be waking up hungry?

This is highly unlikely at the age of nine months, although in hot weather some babies may wake up thirsty and genuinely need a drink. Your son needs the comfort of milk to make the transition from waking to sleeping, rather than the food value. You can help him get back to sleep without disturbing you, however. Stop giving him milk when he wakes, and give him the minimum comfort necessary to settle him instead. Go in every five or ten minutes to repeat the process. Eventually, over a period of several nights, he should stay settled, as long as you and your partner are both consistent .

Why have I been told my baby shouldn't have a bottle after she's 1 year old? she's 10 months now, and still very attached to her bottle, though she can drink from a cup as well.

It's probably sensible to aim for a phasing out of bottles at around the age of a year. Toddlers, like your daughter, get progressively keener on their bottles, and there's a tendency to carry them around with them, taking a swig more or less round the clock. That's fine as long as the contents are plain water, which is the only thing that won't harm teeth or damp down their appetite, but few toddlers drink water. The result can be what dentists call 'nursing bottle caries', severe decay affecting the front teeth because of frequent contact with sweet liquids, including milk. There's also a concern that toddlers can drink a great deal of milk or juice in this way, leaving them too full for other foods.

If your daughter has a bottle after she's 1 year old, don't let her carry it round. Leave it for meal times only, with an evening bottle as a comfort. Don't let her stay asleep with the bottle teat in her mouth.

What about breastfeeding? When should I stop?

There are no nutritional reasons for stopping breastfeeding; theoretically, you could go on forever, and in other societies mothers feed for several years. Breast milk is always a nutritious drink, and it can have a useful function when an older baby or toddler is ill – it may be the only food or drink a sick child will accept.

Many mothers decide they want to stop before their baby does, however. If this applies to you, you may find it's easier to cease breastfeeding before your baby becomes a toddler, simply because babies are easier to distract from what they want than toddlers are, and some toddlers become very fond of breastfeeding. Offer cuddles, drinks from a cup, snacks, at a time when you'd normally breast-feed. You may want to keep up an evening feed for a while, if it's a quick and easy way of getting your baby off to sleep.

7 Your toddler – one to three years

The majority of toddlers are well on the way to joining in with most of the food you eat, and they're growing and developing well on a reasonably wide range of foods.

You no longer need to be so concerned about salted or spiced food at this stage. There are some health grounds to avoid excess salt in the diet, but the main anxiety with babies and toddlers is that too much salt can overload the kidneys. Long before any danger level is reached however a healthy toddler will be thirsty, and by now, she can let you know simply by asking for a drink, using whatever signs or words she has.

> **You can now give cheeses, like Brie, and pâtés. These are thought to have a risk of harbouring the bacterium listeria, but healthy babies should be fine, so if you've been avoiding foods like these, it's no longer necessary.**

Hygiene is always important, whatever the age of your family, and the usual sensible rules about cleanliness and hand washing apply. It's especially important to wash your toddler's hands before every meal, and after using the potty or toilet, because children of this age can get very dirty. They also put their fingers in their mouths.

Your toddler can therefore eat more or less the same as you. *The only item you should still avoid is whole nuts.* Give her whole milk instead of the skimmed or semi-skimmed you might have (see p. 55), and don't add sugar to foods and drinks, even if you add it for yourself . Continue being restrictive about sweets and chocolate and other treats (see p. 56).

FOOD FADS

It's not uncommon for a toddler's appetite to vary. Some children actually eat less as they get older, compared to what they ate at around a year or so. Then, they may start eating more, and forgetting about any food fads they may have developed.

Dealing with any sort of fussiness is difficult for parents. As I see it, there are actually three opposing issues fighting for the title of number one worry. You worry that only ever giving her what she wants (in order to fill her up with something, at least) means she has you on a string, manipulating you and enjoying it. You worry that not giving her what she wants is being oppressive and cruel, denying her the chance to develop normal likes and dislikes. You also worry that whatever you do, she'll end up poorly nourished, if not actually starving.

'We found my son was a far better eater on holiday, when we were camping and eating out of doors. We reckoned it was because we had subconsciously decided not to fuss about anything very much, and mealtimes became so much more relaxed.'

There isn't an easy answer, but if what your toddler eats is basically nutritious, even if it's limited in its range and the quantities are small, then it is far better not to make a fuss, and to accept that this is what she eats at the moment. Make some concession to her preferences, without always serving her something different from the rest of the family. If she only wants to eat a small amount, then let her, taking her plate away without comment when she seems to have finished.

Don't let your toddler fill up on biscuits and junk food between meals, though. It's easier to refuse her requests if you have none of these in the house.

THE 'DIFFICULT EATER'

Occasionally, families get into a knot, when the food the toddler accepts is both very obviously limited and poor in nutritional quality.

She won't eat the food she's offered at lunchtime. She whines at about 3 pm for biscuits because she's genuinely hungry. She gets the biscuits, and then is genuinely too full for much tea. She fills up again with an evening bottle. The same thing happens the next day, with everyone becoming heartily sick of one another, and with the tension rising daily.

Try to take the heat out of the situation by serving up a small portion of food you know your child doesn't actually hate, and making mealtimes enjoyable with plenty of chat and good humour. Point out you have no biscuits at all, in a non-threatening, purely informative way. Put up with her resultant hungry whining (she won't starve, promise), and offer a piece of fruit or a drink. Reduce the amount of milk she has, by offering it in a cup or watering it down in the bottle. Stick to your guns, and stay calm.

If you feel your child has a long-standing fad problem or really doesn't eat enough, you can check her weight at the baby clinic. If it's normal, and she's developing well and healthily, you can reassure yourself she's getting what she needs. If it isn't, then you can be referred for more specialist help. Your health visitor may check your child isn't still getting the majority of her calories from milk, and give you ideas on giving other foods if that's the case.

MANNERS – GOOD AND BAD

Parents today no longer feel obliged to impose the rigid table rules of the Edwardian nursery on their children, but there are certain 'behaviour policies' you can teach that make sense.

Consideration for others is the basis for good manners, and that applies at the table, just as in any other situation. It includes consideration for the feelings and sensibilities of the person who prepared the meal, and the comfort of other people sitting at the same table, and who will have to use the room afterwards.

Be flexible. If you're having a lazy, three- or four-course meal with adult friends, you can't expect your toddler to wait 10 minutes or even longer for her dessert. She can leave the table and return to it later.

Adults, too, need to show consideration at mealtimes where toddlers are concerned. Include them in the conversation, and encourage them to join in the chat.

PARTY TIME!

At any time from the age of 1 year, you may well be a host to your child's friends or young relatives at birthday parties and other celebrations.

Keep toddler party food as simple as you can. You may want to indulge your skills in baking and decorating, of course, when it comes to the birthday cake. That's fine, as long as you can bear the fact that hours of work will be destroyed the second you place a knife in your masterpiece to cut that very first slice.

In fact, toddlers are just as happy with any ordinary round or square cake decorated with Smarties or chocolate buttons. Anything else more complicated impresses other parents rather than your child.

Other foods for the party tea should be small, mostly savoury and easily handled. Also, remember the great thing about little children is that most traditional party foods are still a delightful novelty to them. So don't rack your brains for new ideas. The old favourites will be new to them.

Under-twos won't manage to eat things from cocktail sticks without piercing themselves, so don't use them. Paper or plastic plates and cups are more practical than crockery. They won't get broken and there is no washing up to do after the party. Or you could dispense with plates altogether, and have squares of kitchen paper instead. Many children can't manage straws, and very young toddlers will probably want a spouted cup – ask the parents to send one with them if you don't have enough for guests.

'It helps to get as much adult help as you can when you're organising a party. Looking after a group of under-threes is really hard work. It's especially important they help you watch over the eating. Don't let them all sit in the other room, gossiping over a bottle of wine!'

Party food ideas

For young toddlers

Prepare a selection of mini-sandwiches without crusts; sausages; cubed cheese and pineapple chunks; sliced fresh and dried fruit; tiny fancy buns; chocolate fingers (bought). Fresh fruit juice to drink, with ice cubes as an extra attraction.

For toddlers around the age of 1 year try bowls of finger foods, and tiny jellies in moulds. The jellies will have to be spoon-fed.

For older toddlers

Small, bite-sized bits of food are good. Here's a selection of quick ideas.

○ Nine tiny sandwiches from one round, by slicing it into three one way and three the other to make nine rectangles. Don't choose messy fillings. Ones to try: marmite, cream cheese and cress; ham; scrambled egg; tuna. Reckon on two to three rectangles each.

○ Fish fingers (chopped into three) and chicken nuggets and mini-kievs are popular. So are mini-pizzas, made with toast covered with sliced tomato, sprinkled with oregano and grated cheese and grilled.

○ To make fruity bites, mince a pack of dried fruit salad and shape into small balls and chill.

○ Slice mini Swiss rolls into four rounds, top with a little melted chocolate or glacé icing and decorate with a small sweet.

○ Name biscuits. Pipe a name on a plain biscuit, one per child, using melted chocolate or glacé icing.

○ Bowls of seedless grapes, apple slices and chunks of banana, brushed with lemon juice to prevent browning.

YOUR CHILD AWAY FROM HOME

Some fussy children eat hardly anything in other people's houses. The taste, smell, look of the food is so different (to them) that they're put off.

Try to encourage your child to be sociable and to eat something, without insisting heavily. At this age, you can still explain to your host that your child probably isn't very hungry, without risking any hurt feelings.

YOUR QUESTIONS ANSWERED

My daughter enjoys most fruit, and she has two or three cups of apple juice a day. My problem is she suffers from something the family doctor has diagnosed as toddler diarrhoea. Should I change her diet?

Toddler diarrhoea is quite common, and it's only a health problem in a few cases. Presumably your doctor feels your daughter is healthy, and not losing weight as a result of the diarrhoea, so you don't need to worry. The diarrhoea, really more accurately, loose and frequent stools, is a nuisance for you, but you can be fairly certain that your daughter will grow out of it as she gets older. It's thought to be caused by a simple immaturity in the gut, which resolves itself in time.

If you've noticed that a lot of fruit makes your daughter's diarrhoea worse, then you could give her less. However, it's possible she would react in the same way whatever her favourite foods were, and it's a shame to stop her eating something she enjoys, and which will otherwise do her no harm.

My childminder gives my daughter sweets every day. I've tried to remonstrate with her, but she says she doesn't want to leave my daughter out of things. The other child she looks after has them, and her mother doesn't object.

This isn't so much a food issue as one that reflects your rights as a parent. If the childminder is one you like in all other respects, then you could have a word with the other mother and get her agreement to stick to fruit or sugar-free snacks at the minder's. She can always give her child sweets herself if she wants to. If this does no good, then think about changing your childminder to one who listens to what you want. Most of them do!

What do you do about grandparents who give in all the time? My mother and father see us a lot at weekends, and they help out with babysitting and so on. I can't help getting annoyed, however, because when my daughter eats with them, they let her behave very badly, especially over food. She has pudding even though she hasn't finished her first course, and there's no attempt to get her to stay at the table. My mother tends to spoonfeed her, too, which she thinks is just great.

You can't change your grandparents like you can your childminder! It may help to remember your parents are acting this way out of love for their grandchild, and that it's traditional for grandparents to be more indulgent than parents. Your daughter won't be harmed by learning that different people have different standards, as long as you and your partner are consistent about what you regard as important in your home. You could decide what aspects you feel you want to concentrate on, and pointedly insist on them when you are eating with them and your daughter, so they'll get the message. Forget about the rest.

I find it very hard to stay calm and unworried when it comes to food fads. There have been times when I've been at breaking point. My daughter has half a slice of toast (perhaps) at breakfast with a cup of milk. She may then have something like half a fish finger and a tiny spoon of baked beans and a drink of apple juice for lunch. Tea is a cup of milk, and sometimes nothing, sometimes a couple of spoons of yoghurt or banana. Then she has another cup of milk at bedtime. She's 15 months old, and I can't get her to eat any more than that. She just closes her mouth and screams to be let out of her high chair.

It's hard to ignore things when you feel your daughter is actually doing herself harm, but her diet sounds fine, even though there's not a lot of it, as you suggest. If you've had her weight and health checked, it's probably enough for her. Make sure that she gets her vitamin drops daily.

Her meal-time behaviour is not really a nutritional problem, but it would be better if things were happier for both of you. Your daughter may prefer feeding herself, and you may find this more relaxing than trying to coax her mouth open. Take her out of her high chair, so she doesn't feel restricted. She may just be able to sit on a chair with cushions, if someone's always there to steady her. Give her small quantities so she doesn't feel she's being manipulated into taking more than she wants, and casually offer her more if she finishes what's on her plate.

8 Recipes

FROM FIRST TASTES TO FAMILY MEALS

The introduction of first foods into your baby's milky diet is a real milestone in her development, and a radical change in her way of feeding. As she becomes accustomed to taking food from a spoon rather than sucking, her pleasure in eating semi-solid food will increase. It won't be long before she'll be eating meals at the table with the family, though her table manners may take some time to refine! This chapter provides ideas for first tastes right up to meals which all the family can enjoy, with some tips on maximising your baby's nutrition.

A note on nutrition

In the first couple of years you should be aware of a few important nutritional concerns.

Iron

Apart from the need to minimise sugar consumption which has already been discussed, try to ensure that you provide a range of foods which contain iron. Without sufficient iron children can develop anaemia and suffer a setback in their physical and mental development. The best sources of iron are found in red meat and offal such as liver. Other sources include fortified breakfast cereals, lentils, dried apricots, wholemeal bread, canned sardines and baked beans. Vitamin C helps the body absorb iron so offering a drink of diluted unsweetened orange juice with a meal boosts the amount of iron absorbed. On the other hand, tannin - found in tea - binds iron, so should not be given to toddlers. Several of the recipes in this chapter are excellent sources of iron and you should try to include them at least once a week.

Fibre

A high fibre, low fat diet is fine for adults but totally unsuitable for the under fives. Fibre fills up little tummies and this can mean that they are full before they have consumed all the energy and nutrients they need. Be cautious about the number of times a week you serve pulses and wholegrain cereals. It is better to provide a mixture of ordinary and wholegrain cereals and pasta so that your baby becomes accustomed to the taste of both. **Never** add bran to a baby's or toddler's diet and limit - or avoid giving - high fibre breakfast cereals for the under twos.

Fat

We are being encouraged to cut down on the amount of fat we eat. However, this advice doesn't apply to children under two who need the concentrated source of energy fat provides. Buy full-fat yogurts, fromage frais and cheese for your toddler and if you are using low fat products when cooking for the family, make sure that your toddler has a reasonable sized portion. After the age of two you can gradually introduce lower fat products into your child's diet so that by the time she is five she is having a healthy, lower fat diet like the rest of the family.

Try to use spreading fats and oils that are low in saturated fatty acids and high in mono or polyunsaturated fatty acids. Olive and rapeseed oils contain monounsaturated fatty acids and sunflower and soya oils tend to be high in polyunsaturated fatty acids. Avoid using the very low fat spreads for your baby or toddler.

Salt

Don't use salt when cooking food for a baby. If you are making a meal for the whole family you can always add a little salt at the table. Some foods are high in salt and should be limited or avoided. These include stock cubes, soy sauce, and some yeast or meat extracts.

Which milk for cooking?

In the early months of weaning you may want to add your baby's usual milk, whether expressed breastmilk or formula. Its familiarity and sweetness will encourage your baby to try the food. You can continue using it as long as you wish, but many people prefer to swap to whole cow's milk after six months or a year. Don't forget, though, that cow's milk isn't suitable as a main drink until your baby is one year old.

A note on portions

Your baby's appetite may vary enormously in the first few months of feeding. The portions given in the recipes here are very approximate; you may find your baby loves a particular recipe and eats most of it, whilst refusing another. Try a variety of different recipes and make a note of those that are successful.

You will find that the amount of food cooked in first meals is quite small, but it may still be too much for your baby to eat at one meal. If you are freezing food for future meals, purée the meal whilst the baby's portion cools and spoon the purée into ice cube trays. Cover with film and freeze as soon as it is cool enough. This will ensure maximum vitamin retention.

STAGE ONE: TASTERS

These first tastes are literally that, not helpings or meals. They get your baby used to taking food from a spoon rather than sucking and you can try them at the end of a breast or bottle feed.

Baby rice is often used as a first food, mixed with baby milk. Some babies love it, whilst others prefer a fruitier introduction to solids.

- Try purées of cooked dessert apple or pear.
- Make a thin porridge from baby rice or rice flakes and baby milk.
- Mash a very ripe banana (a black speckled skin shows it is really ripe).

Banana rice

Preparation time: 5 minutes

Small piece of very ripe banana
1-2 teaspoons baby rice

1. Mash the banana to a smooth purée.
2. Stir in a teaspoon or so of baby rice.

Baby mash

Preparation time : 5 minutes
Cooking time　　: 15 minutes

　1 small potato
　Baby milk

1. Scrub the potato, removing any blemishes, and halve.
2. Boil gently until soft, about 10-15 minutes. Cool slightly and skin the potato.
3. Purée the potato with baby milk to make a smooth cream.

Vegetable purée

Preparation time : 5 minutes
Cooking time　　: 15 minutes

　1 small potato
　1 small carrot

1. Scrub the potato, removing any blemishes, and cut in half.
2. Peel the carrot and cut in half lengthwise.
3. Cook the vegetables in unsalted boiling water until just soft.
4. Peel the potato and purée the vegetables, using a little of the cooking water or baby milk as required.

Dried apricot cream

Dried apricots are a good source of iron, calcium and beta-carotene, and babies love their sweet taste.

Preparation time : 5 minutes
Cooking time　　: 15 minutes

　Few dried apricots
　Baby rice or baby milk

1. Pour boiling water over the apricots in a sieve.
2. Place the apricots in a small saucepan and cover with cold water. Bring to the boil and simmer until tender, about 10-15 minutes.
3. Purée the apricots using a little cooking liquid if required, and sieve.
4. Stir in the baby milk or baby rice to taste.

Parsnip and carrot purée

Preparation time : 10 minutes
Cooking time : 15 minutes

   1 carrot
   1 parsnip

1. Peel, top and tail the carrot and parsnip, and dice.
2. Place in a saucepan and pour over enough boiling water to just cover. Bring to the boil, cover, and simmer for 15 minutes or until the vegetables are soft.
3. Drain the vegetables, reserving some liquid.
4. Purée with 1 tablespoon of the cooking liquid.

Pumpkin purée

Preparation time : 10 minutes
Cooking time : 7 minutes

   150g (6oz) pumpkin

1. Peel and remove the seeds and stringy bits from the pumpkin.
2. Cut into 2cm/³/4in. pieces and place in a microwave dish.★
3. Add 2 tablespoons of water, cover and cook for 7 minutes or until the pumpkin is tender.
4. Cool and purée.

★*Alternatively, steam the pumpkin until tender - around 10-15 minutes.*

STAGE TWO: FIRST MEALS

Once your baby has become used to taking food from a spoon, add a few more flavours to her diet. You could try a range of different fruit and vegetable purées, and introduce soft cooked lean meats and poultry or lentils.

It is still too early to introduce any cow's milk or cow's milk products, eggs, or wheat. Wait until your baby is six months old. If your family has a history of eczema, asthma, coeliac disease or other known food intolerance ask your dietitian or health visitor for advice before giving your baby foods which might provoke a reaction. These include cow's milk, eggs, citrus fruit, wheat, shellfish and nuts. The longer you can delay their introduction, the smaller the risk of your baby reacting to the foods.

Carrot soup

(2-3 portions)
Preparation time : 5 minutes
Cooking time   : 10 minutes

   2 small carrots
   1 teaspoon chopped fresh parsley

1. Peel and slice the carrots and boil until just soft, about 10 minutes.
2. Purée with the parsley, adding cooking liquid as required to make a thick soup.

Variation
Add a little baby milk.

Dhal

Lentils provide iron. Serving this with vitamin C-rich broccoli purée would maximise iron absorption.

(2-3 portions)
Preparation time : 5 minutes
Cooking time   : 25 minutes

    50g (2oz) red lentils

1. Check the lentils for stones and rinse in cold water in a sieve.
2. Boil three cups of water and add the lentils. Bring back to the boil, skim, then boil rapidly for 10 minutes.
3. Lower the heat and simmer for 15 minutes to a soft purée, stirring occasionally to prevent sticking.
4. Purée the dhal.
5. Serve with baby rice and a green vegetable purée.

Vegetable dhal

(2-3 portions)
Preparation time : 8 minutes
Cooking time   : 25 minutes

    50g (2oz) red lentils
    A small piece of leek (3-4 cm/1^1/$_2$in)
    1 small potato

1. Cook the lentils as above.
2. Shred and rinse the leek.
3. Peel and slice the potato and cook in boiling water.
4. After it has been cooking for 5 minutes, add the leek and continue cooking until both are soft, about 7-8 minutes.
5. Purée the vegetables with the lentils, adding a little cooking liquid if required.

Spring green purée

This purée is full of vitamins and minerals. Cool and freeze it quickly to keep the vitamin content high.

(Sufficient portions to freeze some)
Preparation time : 5 minutes
Cooking time   : 25 minutes

   1 medium potato
   Half a bunch of watercress, washed and finely chopped
   100g (4oz) mixed green vegetables (green beans, broccoli, spring cabbage)

1. Peel and halve the potato, and boil in unsalted water.
2. After 5 minutes add the watercress to the pan.
3. Roughly chop the other vegetables and cook in a separate pan, or steam over the potatoes.
4. When all the vegetables are tender, drain and purée until smooth.

Summer stone fruit

When peaches and nectarines are in season, make fruity summer purées for your baby. Try freezing the plum purée for use later in the season.

(1-2 portions)
Preparation time : 10 minutes
Cooking time   : 5-7 minutes

   Use any of the following ripe fruit:
   1 peach
   1 nectarine
   2-3 plums
   2-3 apricots

1. Wash the fruit and plunge into a bowl of boiling water.
2. After a minute remove them, rinse in cold water and peel. If pieces of skin are difficult to remove, return the fruit to the boiling water for a few more seconds.

3. Place the peeled fruit in a saucepan with a little boiling water and simmer for about 5 minutes until it is tender.
4. Remove the fruit and stone it.
5. Boil the cooking liquid until only a tablespoon remains and purée the fruit with this.

Note: Adding a little ripe banana will sweeten a sour purée.

Variations
Add baby milk.
Add baby rice to the purée.

Ground rice pudding with paw paw purée

Paw paw is a delicately flavoured fruit and ideal to sweeten this rice pudding. You could use other fruits in season if you prefer. The rice will keep in the fridge for a couple of days but purée the fruit when required.

(2-3 portions)
Preparation time : 10 minutes
Cooking time   : 5 minutes

　　10g (1 heaped teaspoon) ground rice
　　125ml (5fl oz) baby milk
　　1/4 small paw paw, peeled and deseeded

1. Mix the rice with a little of the milk. Heat the remaining milk until almost boiling, then pour onto the rice, stirring well.
2. Return the whole mixture to the pan and heat gently, stirring all the time until the mixture has thickened.
3. Pour into two serving bowls and allow to cool slightly.
4. Purée the pawpaw until smooth and serve with the ground rice pudding.

Cod and vegetable dinner

(2-3 portions)
Preparation time : 5 minutes
Cooking time   :10-15 minutes

> 1/2 small portion (approx. 45g/1 1/2–2oz) of frozen cod, haddock
> or coley, defrosted
> 1 floret of cauliflower, quartered
> 1 tablespoon frozen peas

1. Check the fish for bones and steam on a covered, greased,
   heatproof plate over a pan of water for 10-15 minutes, or
   microwave cook on 'high' until just tender, about 2-3 minutes.
2. Place the cauliflower and frozen peas in a saucepan, just cover with
   boiling water and cook for 5 minutes or until the vegetables are
   just soft.
3. Drain the vegetables and purée the fish, peas and cauliflower
   together until smooth.

Avocado and banana mash

This is an ideal meal to make when you are out. All you need is ripe
fruit and a fork.

Preparation time : 3 minutes
Cooking time   : none

> 1/4 ripe avocado
> 1/4 ripe banana

1. Mash the fruit together until really smooth and creamy.

Variations
For an older baby, mash in some cottage cheese.
For a toddler tea, use the mixture as a sandwich filling.

Sweet potato and broccoli purée

Preparation time : 10 minutes
Cooking time   : 25 minutes

   $1/2$ medium sweet potato
   4 florets broccoli

1. Peel the potato and cut into 1 cm/$3/4$ in. dice.
2. Cook the potato in boiling water for 25 minutes or until tender.
3. Add the broccoli after about 15 minutes.
4. Drain the vegetables, cool a little and purée until smooth.

Variations
Cook a mixture of sweet and ordinary potato, or add parsnip.

STAGE THREE: 6 TO 9 MONTHS

You can now use a wide range of different foods in your baby's diet, but still try to avoid adding unnecessary sugar or salt to foods. Give a few foods as finger foods. Your baby will enjoy chewing on them, but take care with raw vegetables – small pieces can break off and cause choking.

As new foods are added to the diet you can also start to adjust the texture of the foods to include a few small lumps.

   ○ Make purées from lean chicken, turkey, liver, fish or lean red meat.

   ○ Give hard-boiled egg slices as a finger food.

   ○ Wheat based foods such as pasta, bread, breakfast cereals, semolina, cous cous and flour are all acceptable now.

   ○ Make purées from lentils, aduki or mung beans.

   ○ Squeeze an orange and dilute with 4 parts boiled water for a mealtime drink.

   ○ Cow's milk can now be used in cooking but is not advised as a main drink until one year. Using dairy products such as cheese, fromage frais, and yogurts will ensure a good supply of calcium and protein. Choose full fat products and experiment by adding your own fruit purée to unsweetened yogurt or fromage frais.

○ When raspberries and strawberries are in season, rinse, mash and sieve them. They're bound to be popular with your baby.

○ Offer pieces of peeled apple or pear, seedless grapes, or segments of satsuma as finger foods.

○ Salt free rice cakes and breadcrusts make useful finger foods.

○ Cooked, filled pasta is a useful food when you are on the move.

Beetroot soup

Babies will enjoy the sweet taste of this vividly coloured soup. It makes enough for four adult portions plus one for baby. It can be served hot or cold.

Preparation time : 30 minutes
Cooking time   : 30 minutes

450g (1lb) raw, round-shaped beetroot
Half a small leek or 2–3 spring onions, chopped and rinsed
400g (15oz) can tomatoes, drained
4 tablespoons plain full fat yogurt, sour cream, smetana or fromage frais

1. Scrub the beetroot carefully, taking care not to break the skin. Leave the tails on and about 5cm (2") of the stalk.
2. Place the chopped leek or onions, tomatoes and beetroot in a large pan and just cover with cold water.
3. Cover and bring to the boil, then simmer until you can push off the beetroot skin with your finger, about 30 minutes.
4. Drain through a sieve into a bowl, and allow to cool a little.
5. Top, tail and skin the beetroot and shred in a food processor. Mix with the drained onions and tomatoes.
6. Purée a portion for baby, serving with a blob of yogurt.
7. For the family, add the cooking liquid to the vegetables and serve with the yogurt or alternative.

Chicken and vegetable casserole

This chicken dish will serve six adult portions or make a good number of baby meals. Chicken is easy for a baby to chew and digest and its bland flavour is usually acceptable.

Preparation time : 15 minutes
Cooking time   : 2½ hours

> 2 kg (4lb) roasting chicken cut into 6 pieces
> 2 large onions, roughly chopped
> 4 medium carrots, peeled and cut into chunks
> 2 outer stalks celery, scrubbed and sliced
> ½ teaspoon dried thyme
> 1 pinch ground mace or nutmeg
> A few parsley stalks
> Freshly ground black pepper

1. Preheat the oven to 220°C, 425°F, gas mark 7.
2. Place all the ingredients in a large casserole dish and cover with water. Place on the lid.
3. Cook for 20 minutes before reducing the heat to 150°C, 300°F, gas mark 2.
4. Cook for 2 hours or until the chicken is tender.
5. Carefully pour off some of the stock and skim off the fat.
6. Cook a green vegetable in this chicken stock.
7. For baby's dinner, skin some of the white meat and purée with a few pieces of vegetable and a teaspoon or so of the cooking liquid.
8. Serve with the green vegetable and some freshly mashed potatoes.

Chicken liver casserole

If you have saved some of the chicken stock from the casserole you can use it to cook other dishes such as this liver casserole. Liver is the best source of iron and an occasional portion will supply your baby's needs.

(Sufficient portions to freeze some)
Preparation time : 10 minutes
Cooking time   : 20 minutes

    40g (1¹/₂oz) white leek or mild onion, finely chopped
    1 bayleaf
    1 teacup of chicken stock or water
    125g (4oz) frozen chicken livers, thawed
    1 teaspoon freshly chopped parsley

1. Simmer the onion or leek and bayleaf in the water or stock until tender, about 10 minutes.
2. Add the livers, and cook for another 10 minutes until the liver is just cooked. (Their centres should have just turned from pink.)
3. Discard the bayleaf and add the parsley. Purée until smooth.
4. Serve with a purée of potatoes and peas. (See next recipe.)
5. Alternatively, purée the liver, potatoes and peas together.

Potato and pea purée

(2-3 portions)
Preparation time : 10 minutes
Cooking time   : 15 minutes

    1 small potato
    1 tablespoon frozen peas

1. Peel and boil the potato in unsalted water until almost tender.
2. Add the frozen peas and bring back to the boil.
3. Turn off the heat and allow to stand, covered, for 6 minutes.
4. Drain and purée the peas and potato in a little baby milk.

Fruity fish

Citrus flavours complement this mild tasting fish. You can sing 'Oranges and Lemons' whilst you serve it!

(2-3 portions)
Preparation time : 5 minutes
Cooking time   : 15 minutes or less

50g (2oz) whiting fillet, skinned (or you can do this at the end of cooking)
Squeeze of lemon juice
2 tablespoons freshly squeezed orange juice
Knob of unsaturated margarine
1 small cooked peeled potato

1. Place the fish on a greased heatproof plate, pour over the fruit juices and cover.
2. Either steam over a pan of boiling water for 15 minutes or cook on 'high' in a microwave oven for 2-3 minutes.
3. Flake the fish, checking for bones, and boil the juices in a pan with the margarine or butter until slightly reduced in volume.
4. Use the juices to purée the cooked potato and serve with the flaked fish.

Spiced apple pudding

(1 adult or 4 baby portions)
Preparation time : 5 minutes
Cooking time   : 10-15 minutes

1 dessert apple
A pinch of cinnamon
Tiny grating fresh nutmeg
1 heaped teaspoon full fat yogurt, fromage frais or smetana

1. Peel, core and slice the apple.
2. Place in a small saucepan with the spices and add just enough water to cover the apple.
3. Cook gently until soft. Remove the apple and boil down the juices until less than a tablespoon remains.
4. Purée the apple in the juice and serve with a blob of yogurt on top.
Note: If the apple is a little sour, add a small piece of mashed banana to the purée, or add a chopped date whilst the apple is cooking.

Variation
Use pears cooked with a pinch of ground cloves.

Fish and sweetcorn chowder

(2 portions)
Preparation time : 8 minutes
Cooking time   :10 minutes

45g (2 in. piece) cod fillet
100ml (3^{1}/$_{2}$fl oz) milk
2 tablespoons sweetcorn

1. Check the fish for bones.
2. Place the milk, cod and sweetcorn in a saucepan and slowly bring to the boil.
3. Cover and simmer for 10 minutes, stirring occasionally.
4. Cool slightly and purée to the desired consistency.

Crispy topped shepherd's pie

(2 adult portions plus 1 baby portion)
Preparation time : 15 minutes
Cooking time   : 30 minutes

225g (8oz) lean mince
10cm (4 in.) piece of leek, finely chopped
1 small carrot, grated
5 tablespoons water
450g (1lb) potatoes
2 tablespoons milk
1 teaspoon unsaturated margarine

1. Brown the mince in a heavy saucepan for 3-4 minutes, stirring constantly.
2. Stir in the leek and cook for 2 minutes.
3. Add the grated carrot, stir and cook for 2 more minutes.
4. Add the water, cover and simmer for 20-25 minutes until the meat is tender.
5. Meanwhile, peel and halve the potatoes and cook in boiling water until just soft, 15-20 minutes.
6. Drain, add the milk and margarine and mash until smooth and creamy.

7. Preheat a grill and grease an ovenproof dish.
8. Spoon the meat into the dish and top with the potato.
9. Place under the hot grill until golden brown, about 5 minutes.
10. Take out a portion for baby and purée or mash if required.

Pear and prune fool

(3 portions)
Preparation time : 7 minutes
Cooking time   : 5 minutes

> 3 drained canned prunes (or 3 dried prunes, soaked in hot water
> until soft)
> 1 ripe pear, peeled and chopped
> 1 tablespoon water
> 2 heaped tablespoons Greek yogurt

1. Remove the stones from the prunes and chop roughly.
2. Place the prunes, pear and water in a saucepan and heat gently
   until soft.
3. Drain off any excess liquid, purée and cool.
4. Fold the purée into the yogurt, spoon into small bowls and chill
   until required.

Variation
Use dried apricots or peaches. Add a little ground cinnamon to the
fruit.

Chocolate and banana pudding

(2-3 portions)
Preparation time : 5 minutes
Cooking time   : 5 minutes

> 1 heaped teaspoon cornflour
> 1/3 teaspoon cocoa powder
> 100ml (3 1/2fl oz) milk
> 1/2 ripe banana

1. Mix the cornflour and cocoa with a little milk to form a paste.
2. Heat the remaining milk until almost boiling, then pour onto the cocoa mixture, stirring well.
3. Return to the saucepan and heat gently, stirring all the time, until the sauce thickens. Pour one portion into a bowl and allow to cool. Save the remainder for another meal.
4. Mash the banana and mix into the portion in a bowl.

Note: If you are saving the extra for another meal, add the mashed banana just before serving.

STAGE FOUR: 9 TO 12 MONTHS

You can now start to introduce a few wholemeal products and chop rather than purée some foods. Starchy foods such as pasta and potato may be manageable without chopping and many babies like to eat them as finger foods. Try a few raw fruits and vegetables, peeling where necessary, and watching that your baby doesn't choke on any small pieces.

Quick cod with cheese and mushroom sauce

(2 adult and 1 baby portion)
Preparation time : 5 minutes
Cooking time   : 10-20 minutes

   50g (2oz) button mushrooms
   Knob of unsaturated margarine
   50g (2oz) cheese grated
   450g (1lb) cod fillet, skinned

   Sauce:
   20g (³/₄oz) flour
   20g (³/₄oz) unsaturated margarine
   Bayleaf
   300ml (¹/₂pt) milk
   Pinch of ground nutmeg or mace
   Freshly ground black pepper

1. Wipe the mushrooms and chop very finely. Heat the margarine in a frying pan and sauté the mushrooms until soft, about 3-4 minutes. Keep to one side.
2. Make a quick white sauce by whisking together the flour, margarine, bayleaf and milk over a medium heat until the sauce thickens.
3. Remove from the heat and add the seasoning. Discard the bayleaf.
4. Mix two tablespoons of the sauce with the mushrooms.
5. Add the cheese to the remaining sauce.
6. Meanwhile place the fish on a greased heatproof plate and steam over a pan of boiling water for 15-20 minutes. Alternatively, place the fish in a microwave proof dish and cook on 'high' for 4-5 minutes until you can flake the fish with the point of a sharp knife.
7. Check the fish for bones.
8. Serve the fish on a bed of the mushroom sauce, coated with the cheese sauce.
9. Serve with mashed potato and peas or green beans.
10. Your baby may enjoy eating flakes of fish with her fingers.

Tuna fish cakes

These fish cakes should make enough for 2 adult or 6-8 baby portions. The mixture can be frozen either uncooked or once cooked.

Preparation time : 15 minutes
Cooking time   : 20 minutes

150g (6oz) potatoes
2 teaspoons tomato purée
Freshly ground black pepper
1 spring onion, finely chopped
210g (7oz) can tuna in tomato sauce
Wholewheat flour

1. Boil the potatoes, cool slightly then skin and mash.
2. Stir in the tomato purée, pepper and onion.

3. Drain and mash the tuna and stir into the potato, adding a little of the tomato sauce to moisten.
4. Divide the mixture into 8 portions and with floured hands roll each into a small cake.
5. Roll each fish cake in flour and flatten slightly.
6. Either 'dry fry' in a non-stick saucepan until the coating is cooked on both sides, or bake on a greased baking sheet at 220°C, 425°F, gas mark 7 for 10 minutes, turning the cakes once.
7. Serve with a salad or green vegetables and a spoonful of thick, plain yogurt.

Variation:
Use canned salmon, removing larger bones and mashing well.
Oily fish, with the exception of canned tuna, is an excellent source of long-chain fatty acids. Try to include one or two portions of oily fish such as mackerel, sardines, pilchards, trout or salmon in the diet every week.

Creamy courgette pasta

The sauce for this pasta can be served on its own or can accompany pasta. Many babies enjoy pasta shapes as finger foods. Buy animal shapes for added interest.

(2 adult and 1 baby portion)
Preparation time : 10 minutes
Cooking time   : 15 minutes

  1 dessertspoon olive oil
  1 small onion, finely chopped
  1 bayleaf
  1 clove of garlic, crushed
  2 courgettes, washed and sliced
  1 tablespoon chopped parsley
  A few chopped fresh basil leaves
  2 heaped tablespoons curd cheese
  125g (4oz) multicoloured pasta

1. Heat the oil and gently fry the onion and bayleaf. After 5 minutes add the garlic and cook slowly, covered, for 10 minutes. If the mixture sticks, add a little water. Discard the bayleaf and turn off the heat.
2. Cook the courgettes in boiling water until soft, drain and mix with the cooked onion.
3. Add the parsley and basil and stir in the cheese.
4. Purée the mixture until smooth, and warm through.
5. Meanwhile, cook the pasta in boiling water until just tender. Drain and serve with the sauce.

Broccoli and chicken pots

(4 toddler portions)
Preparation time : 10 minutes
Cooking time   : 25 minutes

    1 chicken breast fillet, skinned and roughly chopped
    4 small broccoli florets
    2 eggs
    2 tablespoons milk

1. Preheat the oven to 180°C, 350°F, gas mark 4.
2. Grease 4 ramekins or small ovenproof dishes.
3. Place the chicken and broccoli in a food processor and blend until finely chopped.
4. Add the eggs and milk and process until smooth.
5. Spoon into the ramekins and cover with a piece of greased cooking foil.
6. Stand the ramekins in an ovenproof dish and pour hot water around to reach about half way up each pot.
7. Bake for 20-25 minutes until the mixture has set.
8. Serve with mashed potatoes and a home-made tomato sauce. (See meatballs recipe.)

Orangey pea cous cous

Cous cous is very easy to prepare and is a useful variation to rice or potato.

(2-3 baby portions)
Preparation time : Soak overnight plus 5 minutes
Cooking time   : 45 minutes

  50g (2oz) split yellow peas
  2 dessertspoons fresh unsweetened orange juice
  50g (2oz) cous cous

1. Soak the peas overnight in cold water. Drain, cover with fresh water and bring to the boil.
2. Boil for 10 minutes, reduce the heat and simmer until soft, 30-35 minutes.
3. Cool slightly and purée with the orange juice.
4. Five minutes before serving, place the cous cous in a small saucepan and add 100ml (3$^{1}/_{2}$fl oz) boiling water. Heat until boiling then turn off the heat and allow to stand for 5 minutes.
5. Spoon the cous cous and purée into a bowl and serve with a green vegetable.

Blackcurrant oat crumble

This simple pudding is a good source of iron and will be popular with adults as well as children.

(4 baby portions)
Preparation time : 15 minutes
Cooking time   : 12 minutes

  Small can (213g/8-9oz) blackcurrants in natural juice
  50g/2oz rolled oats
  25g/1oz ground almonds
  10g/$^{1}/_{2}$oz sugar
  25g/1oz unsaturated margarine

1. Preheat the oven to 180°C, 350°F, gas mark 4.
2. Lightly grease 4 small ramekins or ovenproof bowls.
3. Divide the blackcurrants between the bowls, adding a teaspoon of juice to each.
4. Place all the dry ingredients in a small bowl and rub in the fat until the mixture resembles breadcrumbs.
5. Spoon over the blackcurrants and bake for 12 minutes or until just turning brown.
6. For larger appetites serve with plain yogurt or fromage frais.

Rich rice pudding

(3-4 toddler portions)
Preparation time : 5 minutes
Cooking time   : 50-60 minutes

> 170g (5oz can) evaporated milk
> Zest of half a lemon, finely grated
> 1-2 teaspoons sugar – optional
> 20g ($^3/_4$oz) pudding rice

1. Preheat the oven to 160°C, 310°F, gas mark 2.
2. Pour the milk into a measuring jug and make up to 300ml ($^1/_2$pt) with cold water.
3. Grease a small ovenproof dish and pour in the milk.
4. Add the lemon rind, sugar if used and pudding rice. Stir well.
5. Place in the oven and cook until the rice is tender, stirring 3 or 4 times during cooking. Alternatively, place the ingredients in a heavy-based saucepan and cook over a low heat for 40-45 minutes until the rice is tender.

STAGE FIVE: 12 MONTHS ONWARDS

Family meals should be suitable for your baby now. She will enjoy eating the same food as you at all her meals, but still make sure you don't add salt to her food. It's all right to use cow's milk (full fat of course) as a drink now, and try to ensure she has at least 350ml ($^1/_2$pt) a day or two servings of cheese, yogurt or fromage frais.

Parsley meatballs in tomato and pepper sauce

Unless you are bringing up your baby as a vegetarian, do include lean red meat in your toddler's meals. These meatballs are a good source of iron and the tomato sauce provides vitamin C. Your toddler may enjoy eating them as finger food.

(2 adult and 1 toddler portion)
Preparation time : 15 minutes
Cooking time   : 20 minutes

225g (8oz) lean minced beef
1/2 medium onion
3 large sprigs fresh parsley
1 egg yolk
Flour
1 tablespoon oil

Sauce:
1 can (400g/14oz) chopped tomatoes
Pinch mixed herbs
1/2 green pepper, finely chopped

1. Place the meat, onion, parsley and egg yolk in a food processor and process to form a smooth mixture.
2. With floured hands make 20 small balls from the mixture.
3. Heat the oil in a frying pan and gently fry the meatballs until lightly browned and cooked through.
4. Make the sauce by heating the tomatoes, herbs and pepper together until the pepper is tender, about 10–15 minutes. Cool slightly and purée.
5. Serve the meatballs in a pool of tomato sauce with rice and a green vegetable.

Special apple pancakes

(4 pancakes)
Preparation time : 10 minutes
Cooking time   : 20 minutes

1 egg
140ml (5fl oz) milk
60g (2oz) plain flour
Knob of unsaturated margarine, melted
Cooking oil e.g. rapeseed oil

Filling:
2 Cox's eating apples
10g/$^{1}/_{2}$oz unsaturated margarine

1. Peel and slice the apples and fry gently in the margarine until softened and slightly brown, about 7-8 minutes.
2. Meanwhile, blend together the egg, milk, flour and melted margarine until smooth.
3. Heat a few spots of oil in a non-stick frying pan and spoon in two tablespoons of batter. Tip so the batter covers the bottom of the pan.
4. When the pancake is lightly browned on one side turn over and cook the other side. Keep the cooked pancake warm in a clean tea towel.
5. Once all the pancakes are cooked lay the apple slices on one quarter of the pancake, fold in half and half again to make a cornet shape. Turn over the edge of the pancake to show the apple filling.
6. Serve hot with plain yogurt, and a little brown sugar if the apples are not very sweet.
7. Cut up the pancake into bite size pieces for toddlers.

Baked potatoes filled with salmon and dill

(2 adult plus 1 toddler portion)
Preparation time : 5 minutes
Cooking time   : 10 minutes (microwave)
                 : 1 - 1$^{1}/_{4}$ hours (conventional oven)

2 medium baking potatoes
1 small baking potato
105g (3$^{1}/_{2}$oz) cooked fresh salmon or canned pink salmon
$^{1}/_{4}$ teaspoon grated lemon rind
1 tablespoon chopped fresh dill
1 tablespoon Greek yogurt
Black pepper

1. Wash and prick the potatoes with a fork.
2. Bake in a microwave oven for 10 minutes or until tender, or bake in a preheated oven (190°C, 375°F, gas mark 5) for 1–1¼ hours.
3. Drain the salmon and remove any large bones. The smaller ones will purée down if you are making this for a younger child.
4. Mash the salmon with the lemon rind, dill, yogurt and black pepper until smooth.
5. When the potatoes are cooked, slice open and fill with the salmon mixture.
6. Serve with a green salad.

Spicy chick peas

Some toddlers like the spiciness of this dish. If yours doesn't, leave out the spices and replace with a teaspoon of mixed herbs.

(2 adult plus 1 toddler portion)

Preparation time : 10 minutes
Cooking time : 20 minutes

2 teaspoons oil
1 small onion, finely chopped,
1 clove garlic, crushed
1–2 teaspoons ground cumin
1 teaspoon ground coriander
300g (14oz) can chopped tomatoes
400g (14oz) can chick peas, drained and rinsed

1. Heat the oil in a heavy-based saucepan and fry the onion and garlic until softened.
2. Add the cumin and coriander and stir in well.
3. Tip the tomatoes and chick peas into the pan, stir and bring slowly to the boil. Reduce the heat, cover and simmer, stirring occasionally for 15 minutes.
4. Serve with brown rice or as a filling for baked potatoes.
5. For a baby portion, purée 2 tablespoons of the dish.

Variation
Add 2 teaspoons freshly chopped coriander a few minutes before serving.